50
architecture ideas

you really need to know

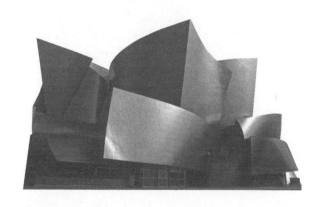

Philip Wilkinson

Quercus

Contents

Introduction

This book is about the key ideas that have underpinned Western architecture from the time of ancient Greece to today. These ideas cover a variety of fields – from technology to decoration, from planning to craftsmanship, and from how to interpret the past to how to build for the future. They include the intellectual sparks that created medieval Gothic, notions that lay behind the idea of the garden city and the technological innovations that produced the skyscrapers.

The first half of the book covers the rich past of architecture from its roots in the style of the Greeks to the revolutionary developments of the late 19th century. It shows how architects and builders created not only a fund of historical styles – from classical to gothic – but also all kinds of ideas – such as prefabrication and the garden city – that interest architects today.

The book's second half begins with the big renewal of the 20th century. The modernism of the early part of the 20th century developed through an explosion of ideas, most of which stripped architecture and design of extraneous decoration and exploited materials such as concrete, glass and steel. From the sculptural forms of the expressionists, to the pared-down, functionalist, concrete-and-glass buildings of the International Style, architects turned their backs on the past. As a result, in the 1920s and 1930s, architectural ideas had never been so rich or so novel.

But great ideas provoke reactions and reinterpretations and the last few decades have seen countless new notions about where architecture should go next. The shocking forms of Archigram and deconstructivism, the irony and allusion seen in postmodernism and the new directions of green architecture have been among the very varied results. They all point to a healthy pluralism in today's architecture. Architecture has rarely had so much variety, or so much potential.

01 The orders

In ancient Greece, probably around the sixth century BC, architects and stonemasons developed a system of design rules and guidelines that they could use in any building whose construction was based on the column. These guidelines later became known as the orders and they went on to have a huge influence, not only in ancient Greece and Rome, but also in later architecture all over Europe, America and beyond.

The orders are most easily recognized by their columns, especially by the capitals – the features that crown each column. The three Greek orders are Doric, with its plain capitals, Ionic, with its capital made up of volutes or scrolls, and the Corinthian, which has capitals decorated with the foliage of the acanthus plant. The simple Doric order was invented first, and some scholars believe that its design, used with such flair by Greek stonemasons, originated in timber building. Doric temples, such as the Heraion at Olympia, go back to c.590 BC. The Ionic appeared soon afterwards, while the earliest Corinthian columns date to the fifth century BC.

To these three the Romans added two further orders, the plain Tuscan and the highly ornate Composite, which combines the scrolls of the Ionic with the acanthus leaves of the Corinthian.

The entablature and proportions There is much more to the orders than the columns and capitals, because what the column supports is also part of the order. Above the column is a lintel made up of three horizontal bands. First comes the architrave, which is usually

timeline

c.590 BC	c.450 BC	447–432 BC
The Heraion, Olympia, is constructed using the Doric order	The temple of Apollo Epicurius, Bassae, is built using the Doric order outside and the Ionic inside, plus a single Corinthian column within	The Parthenon, Athens, the most famous Doric temple, is built

Vitruvius and the orders

The Roman writer Vitruvius produced his handbook *De architectura* (On Architecture) in the first century BC. A practical treatise for architects, it deals in its ten books with many aspects of building – from materials and construction to specific building types. Vitruvius has much to say about the orders, dealing with their origins, proportions, details and application in buildings such as temples. In a memorable passage he describes how the three Greek orders – Doric, Ionic and Corinthian – represent, respectively, the beauty of a man, a woman and a maiden. Vitruvius's book, much reprinted and translated from the Renaissance onwards, had a huge influence on the architects of later centuries when they revived the classical style.

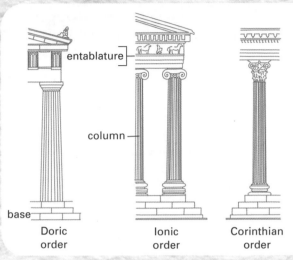

Doric order

Ionic order

Corinthian order

quite plain; then the frieze, which may contain ornate sculpture; and on top of this the cornice, a moulded section that makes the transition between the horizontal part of the order and the roof or gable. Together, these three horizontal bands are called the entablature.

Proportions were also an important aspect of the orders. The height of a column, for example, was expected to be in a certain ratio to its diameter, so it did not look too long and spindly or too short and squat. So the height of a classical Greek Doric column was usually between

427 BC	334 BC	c.48 BC	c.25 BC
The temple of Nike Apteros, Athens, is built using the Ionic order	The Choragic Monument of Lysicrates, Athens, one of the greatest Corinthian structures, is constructed	The Tower of the Winds, Athens, is built in the Corinthian order	Vitruvius writes *De architectura*

❝Thus in the invention of the two different kinds of columns, they borrowed manly beauty, naked and unadorned, for the one [Doric], and for the other [Ionic] the delicacy, adornment, and proportions characteristic of women . . . The third order, called Corinthian, is an imitation of the slenderness of a maiden.❞

Vitruvius, *On Architecture*

four and six times its diameter at the bottom (the columns tapered slightly towards the top). There were also parameters for the depth of the entablature in relation to the column diameter, and so on.

A set of ground rules The orders, therefore, gave ancient architects a complete set of rules from which to design any building based on columns. For the Greeks this meant temples, monuments and other important public buildings. The Romans extended the use of the orders, applying them in different ways to their greater variety of building types, from basilicas to bath houses, but still using the basic design guidelines.

But the orders *were* only guidelines. Different builders and architects used them in different ways, so the scrolls on one Ionic temple differed in detail from those on another, and one craftsman interpreted the acanthus leaves of the Corinthian capital slightly differently from the next. Even the simple Doric order could vary quite a lot in its proportions.

So the architects of ancient Greece and Rome developed a system of architectural design and proportions that could be varied creatively and applied to a range of public buildings. It was a system that served them well, and one that makes buildings in this style instantly recognizable even today.

The origins of the orders The orders may have evolved from construction methods used in carpentry before the Greeks learned to build in stone. The Doric order, for example, features slab-shaped

Key characteristics of architecture

In addition to his work on the orders, Vitruvius also became famous for defining the key qualities at which an architect should aim when designing a building. All buildings, according to Vitruvius should have the qualities of *firmitas* (strength or durability), *utilitas* (usefulness), and *venustas* (beauty). Ever since, architects have kept these qualities in mind when planning their structures.

details called mutules, which look like the ends of wooden rafters poking through the entablature. They further resemble woodwork because they are carved with details called guttae, which look like the pegs used by carpenters in the days before nails. The Roman writer Vitruvius, who wrote at length about the orders, took this view: '. . . in buildings of stone and marble, the mutules are carved with a downward slant, in imitation of the principal rafters.'

It is also possible that early Greek masons were influenced by Egyptian architecture. Some of the columns on certain Egyptian temples, such as the shrine of Anubis at the Temple of Hatshepsut at Deir al-Bahari, are similar in many ways to Doric columns.

A lasting influence However it originated, the method of building using the orders was hugely influential. The Renaissance architects of Italy, the Palladians of 17th-century England, and the neoclassical architects of the 18th and 19th centuries all over the world drew on the Greek orders. The orders represent one of the most enduring ideas in architectural history and there are still neoclassical architects using them in their designs today.

the condensed idea
Ground rules for columns

02 Roman engineering

Roman architecture was distinctive because it brought highly developed engineering skills to bear on large-scale buildings. The Romans made huge strides in engineering, building great aqueducts, large temples, amphitheatres and other structures, some of which are still standing. They did this with the help of materials such as concrete and with innovative structures such as vaults and domes.

The Romans borrowed heavily from the Greeks in many aspects of their culture, and their architecture was no exception. They built temples that looked like Greek temples, surrounding them with rows of columns built according to the orders. But the Romans made advances in engineering and building technology, and it is in these areas that they developed some of the most long-lived architectural ideas.

Roman concrete Probably their most influential idea was concrete, which is easy to think of as a modern invention even though it has been around since Roman times. In fact it was not strictly a Roman idea – both the ancient Greeks and the people of Campania (the part of southern Italy where Greeks and Etruscans had settled) were using mortar in their stone walls at least as far back as the fourth century BC. But the Romans were good at picking up an idea and running with it, and that is what they did with concrete.

timeline

*c.*AD **15**	75–80
Pont du Gard aqueduct, Nîmes, France, constructed	Colosseum, Rome, built

Roman vault-building

Creating the precise curves needed to build a vault is a difficult business, especially if you only have stones and ordinary mortar to build with. You have to put up supporting timber formwork, known as centring, cut each stone very carefully and precisely and then lay the stones carefully on top of the timber. Only long afterwards, when the mortar has set hard, can the centring be removed. With concrete, however, the centring could be much lighter in weight and there was less skill involved in building the vault above it. Since the concrete set quickly, the centring could be removed sooner and the job finished faster.

It was the perfect material for a fast-growing empire, where buildings needed to be put up at speed. When they wanted to build a thick, solid wall quickly, Roman builders used a mixture of rubble mixed with concrete, facing it with brick or dressed stones – the result was cheap, fast to build and very strong. Concrete was also ideal for building the curved shapes – especially those of vaults and domes – that the Romans liked so much. And the Romans developed a way of making a very special kind of fast-setting, water-resistant concrete that was ideal for building bridge piers.

Pozzolana Concrete has been described as a mortar that is mixed with small stones to create a solid, hard mass. It is normally made up of three elements: the aggregate (sand plus stones), the cement (a binding material) and water. The magic was in the binding material, and the Romans discovered an especially effective one – a mixture of lime and a type of volcanic ash known as pozzolana.

100–112	118–28	135	212–16	298–306
Trajan's market, Rome, under construction	Pantheon, Rome, constructed	Temple of Venus and Rome, Rome, built	Baths of Caracalla, Rome, built	Baths of Diocletian, Rome, built

The Pantheon

One of the greatest of all Roman buildings is the Pantheon (below), a temple to all the gods, built in the centre of Rome itself. The Pantheon is a circular building roofed with a dome and the interior of the dome, with its pattern of recessed squares (an effect called coffering) is stunningly beautiful. None of this could have been achieved without the careful use of concrete, the main material of the dome. In particular, the builders varied the aggregate used in the concrete, using heavy travertine and tufa for the foundation and the walls up to the first cornice; lighter brick and tufa for the next level; then brick alone; and finally in the topmost part of the dome an even lighter material, volcanic pumice.

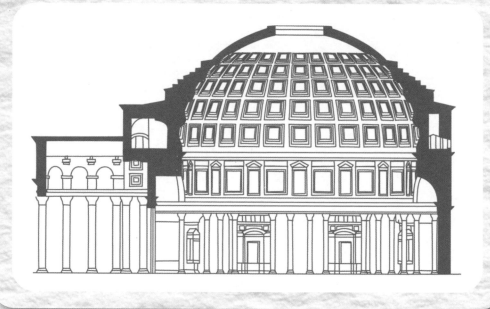

Pozzolana came from the hills around the Bay of Naples, the area known as Puteoli or Pozzuoli. The Romans regarded pozzolana with awe and there are descriptions of its properties in the writings of both Pliny (*Natural History* 35.166) and Vitruvius, who, in his treatise on architecture, points out its key qualities: 'This material, when mixed with lime and rubble, not only furnishes strength to other buildings, but also, when piers are built in the sea, they set under water.' And Vitruvius

> **6... they were naturally devoted to building and that was the favourite extravagance of the rich.9**
>
> **J.C. Stobart,** *The Grandeur That Was Rome*

was right. Roman concrete is so strong that, a thousand years after they were built, and after the masonry facing has been robbed or weathered away, the concrete cores of many Roman buildings still survive.

Spanning rivers So concrete made with pozzolana was ideal for bridge building. This was important because stone bridges were very difficult to build without fast-setting concrete. In fact, most bridges before the Romans were either very small-scale stone-clapper bridges across streams or wooden structures that had a limited life. So Roman concrete transformed bridge building.

Arches and domes But its usefulness went further than this, taking Roman architecture in directions unthought of by the Greeks. In particular, it was ideal for creating structures that were curved. Domed buildings, such as the great temple of the Pantheon in Rome or the vast imperial bath-houses, vaulted buildings such as the Romans' great basilicas and all types of arched structures, were made much more feasible with the use of concrete.

None of these structures was a Roman invention – the Greeks had built domes and vaults before the rise of Rome. But what was significant was the way the Romans extended and developed their use, creating vast domes, such as the one roofing the Pantheon, and huge arched structures. It was the Romans, devoted to building and determined to make ever larger and more magnificent monuments, who made these types of structures into great architectural ideas and developed their huge potential. They transformed the architectural scene.

the condensed idea
Strength through concrete

03 Gothic

In the mid-12th century Abbot Suger of the French abbey of St Denis commissioned a remodelling of his church. The building was constructed in a new way, with pointed arches, large stained-glass windows, high stone vaults and flying buttresses. So effective was this new style that it spread throughout Europe, dominating Western architecture for more than 300 years. It became known as the Gothic style.

In the 12th century a monk called Suger was elected abbot of his monastery of St Denis, north of Paris. He decided to rebuild his church, starting at the east end. He gave the building a new choir and seven chapels radiating around the east end, each with two large, glittering stained-glass windows. The pointed arches, stone vaults, flying buttresses and large colourful windows were the key features of a new style of architecture. Soon, Suger's innovations would be copied all over France and the rest of Europe.

What was the thinking behind Suger's new way of building? The abbot had a love of brightly coloured stained glass, glittering metalwork, jewelled reliquaries and similar objects. For many people, however, such lavish objects of display were inappropriate for a monastery – monks took a vow of poverty, after all. For Suger, though, brightness and light had their roots in Christian theology.

Rooted in the Bible Suger read deeply in the Bible and the writings of the church fathers. He sought out Old Testament descriptions of the Temple of Solomon, writings by saints and accounts

timeline

1122
Suger is elected
abbot of St Denis

1140
The west front of
St Denis is consecrated

by early churchmen that described the spiritual properties of religious imagery. And he no doubt reread biblical passages, such as the one in St Paul's Epistle to the Ephesians, which sees the Christian community as a fellowship with the saints and the household of God himself.

Suger saw his church as an image of God's kingdom. But how was such a place, pervaded by the presence of God himself, to be imitated on Earth? Suger took his cue from Christian writers who portrayed God in terms of his light. So the book of Revelation describes Heaven in terms of rainbow-like light and crystal and the writings of Dionysius the 'pseudo-Areopagite' portray all visible things as lights that reflect the light of God.

Building with light So the abbot asked for a church flooded with coloured light from large stained-glass windows, windows so large that there was virtually no wall left, and so tall that most of the building, from floor to

As the medieval masons mastered the new way of building, they designed larger and larger windows and new ways of dividing up each window into a series of panels (known as lights) into which the glazier could insert stained glass. The design of the stonework, often highly intricate, is known as tracery (because the designs were drawn out in chalk on a tracing floor before being transferred to wood templates that the mason could follow). Tracery became more and more elaborate as the Middle Ages progressed.

"Bright is that which is brightly coupled with the bright, and bright is the noble edifice which is pervaded by the new light."

Abbot Suger

1144	c.1150	1175	1194–1220
Elaborate ceremonies mark the dedication of the new choir at St Denis, which becomes the model for the Gothic way of building	The new cathedral of Notre Dame, Paris, is begun	Rebuilding of Canterbury Cathedral begins: Gothic is well established in England	Chartres Cathedral is built

ceiling, was glass. When the new parts of Suger's church were finished, light flooded into the building from east and west, bathing the whole interior in a brightness unknown in previous churches.

This stunning effect was achieved with a new system of construction. In the previous generation of churches, the arches had been semicircular, like those of the Romans. But at St Denis and the other medieval churches that followed it, the arches, the tops of the windows and the vault ribs were pointed. This made them seem to reach upwards towards Heaven, a powerful symbolic gesture.

Pointed arches have a structural benefit, too. With the old semicircular arches, the width of the opening they span is always exactly twice the height, and this makes them very inflexible when it comes to vaulting. Pointed arches, by contrast, can be designed with different width-to-height ratios, which makes it much easier to vault rectangular and irregular spaces.

Flying buttresses

A cross-section of a typical Gothic cathedral shows how the weight of the stone vault and its outward thrust are held in check by the massive masonry of the flying buttresses on the outside of the building. The flying half-arches of each buttress turn the thrust from an outward-pushing force into a vertical one, sending it down, though the mass of masonry, towards the ground. None of this massive structure is visible from the inside of the building, which is dominated by the pointed arches and large windows.

'Now therefore ye are no more strangers and foreigners, but fellow citizens with the saints, and of the household of God; and are built upon the foundation of the apostles and prophets, Jesus Christ himself being the chief corner stone.'

Ephesins 2: 19–20

A stone skeleton So in Gothic, the stonework becomes an elegant, pointed-arched skeleton made up of pillars, shafts, window mullions and vault ribs. Everything is pointed, and all the moulding profiles match so that the entire structure is harmonious. At wall level the spaces between the skeleton are mostly filled with glass; up in the ceiling, the parts between the ribs are filled with stone. The resulting light-filled interior is enclosed in a structure of almost magical airiness.

But there was a problem. A light network of pillars and shafts is not a very good support for a stone-vaulted ceiling. The weight of the stones up above creates an outward thrust, which tends to push the tops of the walls apart and, left to its own devices, would lead to the collapse of the entire building. The inspired invention of flying buttresses dealt with this structural concern.

A lasting style So the combination of spiritual vision and engineering skill combined to make the Gothic churches of the Middle Ages. This new way of building, so successful at St Denis, spread across France, to England and to the rest of mainland Europe. Masons devised different ways of designing Gothic details, but the style survived, in various modified forms, to the end of the 15th century, and was revived in the 18th and 19th centuries. For many, Abbot Suger's vision still defines what a church should look like.

the condensed idea
Reaching towards heaven

04 Renaissance

The 'Renaissance', coming from the Italian word for rebirth, came about when artists turned their backs on the medieval world and sought a model for their civilization in ancient Greece and Rome. The movement began in Italy, but spread across Europe, transforming architecture as Gothic was left behind and different forms of classicism were taken up in its place.

One of the most far-reaching cultural movements of all time was the Renaissance, which began in Italy when artists, funded and encouraged by a rich class of merchants, aristocrats and guilds, made a break with the recent past and began to revive the classical artistic values of the ancient world. The result was a revolution in painting, sculpture and architecture in the rising Italian cities of the 15th century, first of all in Florence.

A new approach to the classics There was nothing new with studying the ancient world. The literate classes – mainly the priests and monks – had read the ancient writers through the Middle Ages and they had used Latin as the language both of scholarship and of international communication. But they engaged mostly with the philosophical and theological side of the ancient writers. The change in the Renaissance was to read and value these writers and look at their art for its own sake.

In the visual arts, this meant a new naturalism of representation, together with a new 'humanism' – in other words, a stress on the importance of humankind in the scheme of things. This did not mean

timeline

1420–36	1430	1452
Filippo Brunelleschi, dome, Florence Cathedral, constructed	Filippo Brunelleschi, S. Spirito, Florence, begun	Leon Battista Alberti, *De re aedificatoria*, first version published

Organizing Vitruvius

Renaissance readers felt that the text of Vitruvius's book was not very well organized, so most Renaissance writers took what they thought most useful from his work and tried to present it in a more coherent way. Alberti, for example, presented his work *De re aedificatoria* in ten books, in conscious imitation of Vitruvius. But he emphasized certain key ideas of the Roman writer to make his own theories clearer and more consistent. Alberti laid particular stress on the three key qualities that Vitruvius said a building should display: *utilitas* (usefulness), *firmitas* (strength) and *venustas* (beauty).

leaving behind the values of Christianity. Far from it. But it was an acknowledgement that human beings could bring something worthwhile into the world – works of art that were dignified, harmonious, well proportioned and so on.

This more human-based approach was allied with advanced and eye-opening theoretical studies of subjects such as geometrical perspective and proportions. In architecture it meant a return to a version of the classical style, and a new examination of classical writings about architecture, proportions, ornament, construction and allied subjects – especially of the work of the great Roman writer Vitruvius.

Writers and printers The Renaissance coincided with the invention of printing with movable type, and one effect of this was to make editions and translations (and 'corrected versions') of Vitruvius widely available. These added illustrations to Vitruvius's text, making it clearer and effectively updating it, rendering it more relevant to 15th-century needs.

1470	1506	1511	1521
Alberti, S. Andrea, Mantua, begun	Donato Bramante given the commission to remodel St Peter's, Rome	Fra Giovanni Giocondo da Verona, a Franciscan friar, makes a 'corrected' edition of Vitruvius, with woodcuts	Artist and architect Cesare Cesariano makes the first complete translation of Vitruvius

In addition to the translators, many artists, architects and scholars published their own ideas on architecture and building. The first to do this was Leon Battista Alberti, a great architect, writer, painter, mathematician and scholar who also wrote about painting and sculpture. Alberti's *De re aedificatoria* (1452 and further editions) was arranged in ten books (as was Vitruvius's work) and covered subjects ranging from plans and structures to ornament and, of course, the orders. It also promoted ideas such as *decorum* (building in a manner appropriate to a structure's purpose) and *civitas* (civilization based on the city).

Orders and plans Various key elements emerged from these editions of Vitruvius and in books such as Alberti's. Above all, of course, the orders (see pp. 4–7) were described and illustrated to give architects

Vitruvian proportions

The Roman writer Vitruvius had put forward the notion that the orders were related to human form – Doric was manly, Ionic was like a woman and Corinthian like a girl. Renaissance theorists took this further, relating the proportions of the human body to geometry with the 'Vitruvian man'. Vitruvian man was portrayed by many artists – the version by Leonardo da Vinci (right) is the most widely reproduced and most beautifully drawn. His poses and precise proportions vary (his legs sometimes together, sometimes apart, sometimes widely splayed, for example), but whatever the exact geometry he is made to illustrate, his popularity reveals how the human form was central to Renaissance ideals and proportions.

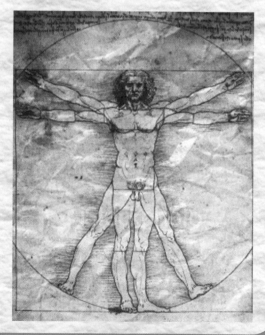

> **... the harmony and concord of all the parts achieved in such a manner that nothing could be added or taken away or altered except for the worse.**
>
> **Alberti, on beauty**

a visual vocabulary for classical buildings. Because Vitruvius was a Roman writer and the Renaissance first flowered in Italy, all five Roman orders (Tuscan, Doric, Ionic, Corinthian and Composite) were shown, not just the original Greek trio.

In addition, sample buildings, reconstructed from the words of the ancients and extant ruins, were illustrated. As with the orders, architects were given a set of models and plans on which to base their own designs – converting an illustration of an ancient temple into a church, for example. Sometimes these illustrations were far from accurate. But their basis in geometry and the combination of plans and perspective views included gave architects plenty to think about and adapt to their own uses.

Italy and beyond This new consciousness of classicism and classical proportions transformed architecture, first of all in Italy. The first great architect of Renaissance Italy was Filippo Brunelleschi, who is most famous for designing the great dome of Florence Cathedral. His other buildings, such as the delicate Pazzi Chapel and the more monumental S. Spirito, both in Florence, are more classical. Alberti is the other great early Renaissance architect, his most famous buildings being the Tempio Malatestiano in Rimini and the cavernous church of S. Andrea, Mantua, which has a west front like a Roman triumphal arch. Buildings such as these proved an inspiration for further generations of Italian Renaissance architects in the late 15th century and beyond, and for builders from further afield as Renaissance ideas spread through Europe during the following decades.

the condensed idea
Classical architecture reborn

05 Palladianism

Andrea Palladio was one of the most influential architects of all time. His distinctive, severely classical style was developed in 16th-century Italy, but it influenced architects all over Europe and in America for more than 200 years. The proportions, symmetry and grand entrance porticoes of Palladian buildings still seem to exude an aura of classical authority.

The architecture of the Renaissance, with its grounding in the orders and the ideas of Vitruvius, dominated the cityscapes of Italy in the 15th century and throughout the 16th. Renaissance architects such as Bramante and Alberti had a huge influence in Italy and beyond, as did Michelangelo, whose buildings formed just a part of his huge achievement. But in the 16th century another architect, Andrea Palladio, came to have a still broader influence.

Architect and writer Palladio was born in Padua and first worked as a stonemason in Vicenza. Here he caught the eye of a humanist aristocrat, Giangiorgio Trissino, who educated him and took him to Rome to study the buildings of the ancient Romans. Back in Vicenza and the surrounding region he was soon designing palaces and country houses for the North Italian nobility. In addition he became a writer, recording the ancient buildings he saw in Rome in *Le antichità di Roma* (the first proper guidebook to the city's Roman remains) and publishing *I quattro libri dell'architettura* (The Four Books of Architecture), which became one of the most influential architectural textbooks of all time.

Like his predecessors Alberti and Bramante, Palladio was a classical architect heavily influence by the ideas of Vitruvius and the buildings

timeline

1556	1570	1579	1616
Palladio's Villa Capra, near Vicenza, begun	Palladio publishes his *I quattro libri dell'architettura*	The Teatro Olimpico, Vicenza, is begun	Inigo Jones begins work on the Queen's House, Greenwich, London

> **"Vitruvius is my master, Rome is my mistress, and architecture is my life."**
>
> **Andrea Palladio**

of ancient Rome. But his buildings had several key features that were widely imitated later – his plans were meticulously symmetrical, his proportions were based on the principles of musical harmony and, since no Roman houses survived for later architects to copy, he created his own special form of house – the villa – with frontages based on Roman temples.

There was a ready clientele for Palladio's buildings in northern Italy. He designed many buildings in Vicenza, from palazzi to the famous Teatro Olimpico, a theatre with a built-in stage set (designed by Palladio's follower Scamozzi) based on a perspective view of an ideal Renaissance city. But most famous were his villas, country houses in the Veneto region of Italy, buildings that were copied widely. He also built churches in Venice. But because of his writings, his influence spread far beyond northern Italy.

The style spreads The first great Palladian was the English architect Inigo Jones. When Jones went to Italy, which he visited twice, he explored the ancient monuments with Palladio's guidebook in his hand. Back in England he determined to bring classical architecture to a London still full of timber-framed houses. Two of his London designs especially, the Banqueting House in Whitehall and the Queen's House at Greenwich, show his success. The Queen's House, in particular, with its rather severe symmetry, pale stone and formal layout, must have shocked Londoners. But after it, English architecture was never the same. In one form or another, classicism remained a powerful force in England until the 20th century.

1619	**1633**	**1725**	**1738**
The Banqueting House, Whitehall, London, is designed by Inigo Jones	Mauritshuis, The Hague, designed by Jacob van Kampen, begun	Lord Burlington designs Chiswick House, London, for his own use	Isaac Ware's English translation of Palladio's *I Quattro libri* published

The villa

Palladio's villas are compact country houses outside Venice, built mostly for the younger sons of Venetian nobles. They were working farms, centred on houses of unsurpassed elegance. The entrance façade of a Palladian villa is dominated by a large columned portico. This is because Palladio had read in Vitruvius that Greek temples were based on house design. So Palladio thought that ancient Greek houses (which do not survive) must have looked like ancient Greek temples (which do) and therefore his own classical houses should be fronted with porticoes. Another key element of villa design was symmetrical planning. This meant that a room on the right was mirrored by an identically sized and shaped room on the left, and so on. Some of Palladio's houses, such as the famous Villa Capra (below), are so symmetrical that they even have an entrance portico on each of the four sides.

Translating Palladio

The Palladian revival was fuelled in part by numerous translations of Palladio's books, which came out in England during the 18th century. The first was by an architect from Venice who settled in England, Giacomo Leoni, whose English translation of Palladio's *I Quattro libri* came out in 1716. But in 1738 a more accurate translation appeared. This was by Isaac Ware, a follower and protégé of Lord Burlington. Ware's accuracy and his connection to Burlington made his translation the one approved by the Palladians in Britain.

Under the auspices of the successful classical architect Elias Holl, Palladian ideas spread to Germany. The style also became fashionable in Holland, in the work of Jacob van Kampen, architect of the Mauritshuis, The Hague, and the grand Town Hall (later the Royal Palace) of Amsterdam. Like Jones and Holl, van Kampen had been to Italy and there he had probably met Vincenzo Scamozzi, an architect who had known Palladio and who completed several of Palladio's works, including the Teatro Olimpico, on the master's death.

These 17th-century Palladians were influential, but the ideas of Palladio has even more impact in the 18th century, especially in Britain, where architects such as Colen Campbell and Lord Burlington were especially attracted to Palladio's villas, and two very close imitations of the Italian's Villa Capra, near Vicenza, were built at Mereworth Castle, Kent, and Chiswick House, London, which Burlington built to show off his art collection. Many other symmetrically planned, severely classical, portico-fronted houses appeared, cementing Palladio's influence in Britain in the first half of the 18th century. Germany and Russia caught the bug of Palladianism from Britain and the movement also influenced Thomas Jefferson, architect and president of the USA. From small beginnings in part of northern Italy, the reach of the Palladian style had become global.

the condensed idea
Symmetry and harmony, porticoes and villas

06 Baroque

In the 17th and early 18th centuries a combination of religious change and the inventiveness of a number of architects in Italy and Central Europe brought about a new kind of architecture. A looser, more dramatic sense of space was combined with freer, often illusionistic decoration, a new sense of lighting and a virtuosic way with curves to produce what we now call the baroque.

The religious movement known as the Reformation swept across Europe during the 16th century. It embodied a questioning of the ideas and practices of the Catholic Church and led to the burgeoning of new Protestant churches, especially in northern Europe. The Catholics responded with a movement that offered some reforms while also reaffirming traditional Catholic beliefs and combining this with a major campaign to bring people back to the church. This movement was called the Counter-Reformation, and art and architecture played an important part in it.

The Counter-Reformation used the arts to bring people nearer to religious ideas and ideals, to increase their emotional involvement with religion and to emphasize the grandeur of God and the stature of the saints. The style that artists adopted to achieve this became known as the baroque.

Baroque space In architecture baroque means above all a new sense of space. Renaissance architecture had been primarily about simple, primary geometry – rooms in the form of cubes or double cubes roofed by hemispherical domes. Similarly, the plan of a typical

timeline

1624–33	1635
Bernini's baldacchino, St Peter's, Rome, popularizes the use of twisted columns	Borromini's S Carlo alle Quattro Fontane, Rome, begun. Its oval dome is patterned with octagons, hexagons and crosses

Trompe l'oeil

The use of *trompe l'oeil* painting was one way in which baroque artists and decorators created a sense of interior space. *Trompe l'oeil* (from French words meaning 'deceive the eye') involves painting scenes that are so realistic that they seem to be real. In baroque churches this device is often used in ceiling painting, where the ceiling seems to become a sky populated with the heavenly host. The cornices around the tops of the walls act as a type of window frame on to this celestial view, but angels, or putti, may lean across it, apparently looking down into the human space below. This kind of decorative effect was a way of bringing heaven closer to the human world, encouraging our emotional involvement, one of the strategies of the Counter-Reformation.

Renaissance building was made up of a series of squares, circles and equilateral triangles.

The architects of the Counter-Reformation, by contrast, created a much more complex, dramatic, three-dimensional geometry. Domes could be oval. Façades, instead of being made up of straight lines, could curve in and out to make patterns unknown in architecture before. Interior spaces had a new fluidity, with much use again made of sensuous curves and, occasionally, of dramatic twisted columns.

1642	1657	1703	1746
Borromini's S. Ivo della Sapienza, another church with a revolutionary dome, is begun	Bernini designs the piazza in front of St Peter's, Rome	Christoph Dientzenhofer's St Nicholas, Prague, Czech Republic, begun	Dominikus Zimmerman's pilgrimage church of Die Wies, near Munich, Germany, begun

These effects were emphasized by unusual lighting effects (shafts of light from high concealed windows, for example) and the use of clever illusions to make space seem more fluid.

The baroque sense of social space drew on similar ideas. The most famous example is the piazza in front of St Peter's, Rome. Its two great curving colonnades, designed by Gianlorenzo Bernini in 1657, form one of the greatest examples of baroque urban space.

Ornament and detail These large-scale spatial effects were mirrored on the smaller scale of ornamental detail. Cornices scrolled this way and that, placing concave and convex curves together. Arches could take on curious, bending shapes. Balconies and baluster rails dipped and bowed in and out. And where traditional geometrical forms, such as the circle, were employed, they were sometimes broken up visually into new patterns. A famous example is the circular dome of the church of S Lorenzo, Turin, designed by Guarino Guarini. This dome is criss-crossed with vaulting ribs and subdivided into segments that are pierced with small windows in odd shapes – pentagons, ovals and circles broken with scrollwork.

Architecture and emotion The effect of the baroque churches of Italy, designed in the 17th century by architects such as Guarini and Francesco Borromini, was to dazzle the eye. Their curious and sometimes bizarre sense of space encouraged an emotional response that was just what the popes wanted, bringing people back to a more immediate, visceral involvement in their religion. Combined with highly charged painting and sculpture – the most famous example is Bernini's dramatic sculpture of the ecstatic St Theresa in S. Maria della Vittoria, Rome – these baroque churches created exactly the new, emotional engagement with religion the church required.

> **Architecture can change the rules of Classical Antiquity and make up new ones.**
> Guarino Guarini, *Architettura civile*

The term 'baroque'

The artists and architects of the 17th and 18th did not describe themselves or their art as 'baroque'. The word originally seems to have been an insult, and has been derived from a term for a rough or imperfect pearl. To classicists, baroque architecture did originally seem like a distortion of pure classicism.

The spread of the idea The baroque style soon spread to France, where architects adopted it for the design of both churches and grand chateaux. During the 18th century it also became popular in Central Europe. In Germany, Austria and the Czech Republic architects such as Jacob Prandtauer, Christoph Dientzenhofer and Dominikus Zimmermann designed baroque churches on the grand scale. In their interiors, enormous arches reach from floor to ceiling, geometry seems to dissolve in a riot of curves and the worshipper is dwarfed by the sheer size of the spaces.

The ornament adds to the effect. Gigantic statues of saints and bishops, swirling ceiling paintings of the heavens and rich gilding abound. Pulpits are set high on the walls so that the congregation must look up. The whole effect is humbling, and slightly disorienting. Although the basic vocabulary of classicism is used – Corinthian columns, architraves and friezes – it is as if the architecture of Greece, Rome and the Renaissance had been held in front of a distorting mirror. This powerful sense of distortion has kept baroque in the public eye, holding its influence on interior design long after the architectural style was current.

the condensed idea
Curves, light and drama

07 The Grand Tour

The custom for young well-to-do Europeans and North Americans to go on a Grand Tour or journey of cultural discovery around Europe was hugely influential on architecture during the 17th and 18th centuries. The Grand Tour helped to define Rome as the cultural centre of the Western world, spread classical ideas and began the tradition of 'culture tourism' that continues today.

From the 17th to the early 19th century, young aristocrats from Britain, Germany and Scandinavia, together with many well-to-do young men from North America, flocked to the towns and cities of southern Europe on the Grand Tour. Their main destination was Italy, although many stopped off in Paris and other places in France en route. In the 18th century, before there were railways or even good roads, travel on this scale was a major undertaking requiring careful preparation, guidance and money. Travelling slowly and stopping often, many Grand Tourists were away for months or even years.

Some travellers, with plenty of money and time, and a sense of adventure, took in still more out-of-the-way places, such as Switzerland or Spain. For a few, such as the restless Lord Byron, yet more far-flung destinations had a stronger attraction – Greece proved an occasional destination for these adventurers, and a few, such as Byron himself, visited Constantinople.

A classical education The principal goal of the Grand Tourists was Italy and especially Rome. Here they hoped to absorb the

timeline

1705

Joseph Addison's *Remarks on Several Parts of Italy,* a popular guidebook, is published

1722

Jonathan Richardson's *An Account of the Statues, Bas-reliefs, Drawings and Pictures of Italy, France, etc* is the first English guide to works of art in continental Europe

Architects on the Grand Tour

Since Inigo Jones travelled to Europe in the early 17th century many architects wanted to go on the Grand Tour and visit buildings such as the château of Vaux le Vicomte (below). Since architects did not usually come from rich families, a young architect wanting to explore Europe would usually attach himself to an aristocratic patron. Robert Adam, architect for Syon House, went to Europe with the Hon. Charles Hope, the younger brother of the man for whom Adam's brother, John, was working on Hopetoun House; James Wyatt travelled with a member of the British embassy to Venice; William Kent, a joiner's son from Bridlington, won the support of some Yorkshire gentry. Others had to travel to Italy under their own steam. James Stuart, for example, walked most of the way to Rome, earning money as he went by painting fans. Such was the appetite of architects to see the buildings of antiquity and of the Italian masters who had drawn inspiration from them.

1797

Mariana Starke begins to write her *Letters from Italy*, an influential guide to the country

1840

The rise of the railway system puts an end to the type of travel that typified the Grand Tour

> **According to the law of custom, and perhaps of reason, foreign travel completes the education of an English gentleman.**
>
> **Edward Gibbon**

atmosphere of Rome and other cities, to look at classical works of art, to learn about architecture and to buy examples of art that they would display in their houses on their return home.

In Rome the Grand Tourists headed for the great classical sites – such as the Forum, the Pantheon and the Colosseum. They sought out the best examples of ancient statuary and they used their connections to gain entry to private houses to view the owners' collections. Most travelled with a tutor, who could steer them in the direction of the best ruins and works of art, and with one or more guidebooks, for information about routes, itineraries and antiquities.

They looked at more recent monuments, too, admiring Rome's baroque planning and Renaissance churches, and perhaps heading off into the countryside to view some of the villas designed by Palladio. Some later Grand Tourists also travelled south to Naples to take in the ruins of Pompeii and Herculaneum, where they could see how the Romans decorated the interiors of their houses as the buildings emerged from their covering of volcanic debris.

Culture shopping All the while, under the guidance of their tutors, the tourists looked out for works of art to bring back home. As well as paintings, classical statues were highly prized, as were engravings by artists such as Piranesi, showing the Roman antiquities they had seen. For those who went to Venice, Canaletto's great paintings of the city were especially popular.

Many Grand Tourists sent crates of paintings, statues, books and engravings back to their homes. Once the new owners of this material had returned home too, there came the challenge of finding somewhere to display it all. In England especially, the art of architecture was seen as a fitting pursuit for a young aristocrat – after all, it was part of the business of running a large estate, which is what many of these people were destined to do for the rest of their lives.

The architectural influence So the Grand Tourists returned home and began to adapt, extend or rebuild their houses – both to accommodate their new collections and to reflect the classical taste they had imbibed. This process was a major factor in which classical architectural ideas were spread across Europe. The fashion in the 18th century for Palladian villas, for example, was fuelled by the Grand Tour. One of the greatest of these, Lord Burlington's house at Chiswick, was designed specifically to house the works of art that Burlington had acquired on his tour.

Later trends towards neoclassicism were similarly inspired by travels in Italy. Robert Adam himself visited Italy, and so was well able to respond to his clients' requests to build not just neoclassical houses, but houses that had bits of antique statuary or even ancient imported columns built into them.

The Grand Tour had a further and deeper impact. It set the agenda for the way the cultural history of Europe has been seen ever since. Millions of culture tourists – less rich but equally eager to seek out their artistic roots – have followed in their footsteps. Rome, Venice and Pompeii (not to mention Paris) have been on the tourist map for north Europeans and North Americans ever since.

the condensed idea
Culture tourism arrives

08 Industrial architecture

The industrial revolution brought new types of building, including factories and warehouses. Although based on older designs for buildings, such as mills, the factories of the 18th and 19th centuries also took design and construction in new directions, especially in designing the structural metal frameworks that prepared the way for the skyscrapers of the 20th century.

In the 18th and 19th centuries the coming of large-scale industry transformed the lives of people all over the Western world. It transformed their architecture too. New building types – factories and warehouses especially – were devised to accommodate the new manufacturing industries and their goods. To build them a new type of builder created a new type of architecture.

The industrial revolution The revolution happened first in Britain because that was where a number of factors came together – cloth production by hand was already well established, fuels such as coal to drive machinery were widely available, technology was developing fast and the British empire supplied both raw materials, such as cotton, and a captive market for finished goods.

The first factories took their power from water, just as the mills of the Middle Ages had done, and they resembled the old mills, too. Their

timeline

1709	1771
Abraham Darby I pioneers the smelting of iron using coke as a fuel	Richard Arkwright builds his pioneering cotton mill at Cronford, Derbyshire

simple, four-square architecture, rows of windows and continuously turning water wheels looked just like their predecessors, although they often had walls of brick or stone. Not surprisingly these early factories were also referred to as mills.

The risk of fire These buildings packed in a large number of machines and a lot of workers. One factory, a silk mill built by John Lumbe in the early 18th century near Derby, was a five-storey building measuring 34 × 12 metres (110 × 39 ft) and accommodating 300 workers. Buildings such as this were often brick-walled, but their interiors contained a lot of timber – wooden beams and columns holding up timber floors; wooden roof trusses supporting the tiles. Combined with the naked flames needed for lighting and the flammable lubricants used in the machinery, they were dangerous places. There were many fires.

Building with iron Fortunately, the industrial revolution had the answer: iron. The iron industry was developing quickly alongside developments in manufacturing. There was a big demand for iron to make machinery, and new techniques of smelting were producing more and better iron. Builders soon started to use the material for construction. The most famous structure to use the material in this way was the bridge over the River Severn at Ironbridge, England. It was built in 1779 and it was the first bridge made completely of iron. Its builder, Abraham Darby, was a member of a dynasty of ironmasters.

> **❝Thy mills like gorgeous palaces arise, And lift their useful turrets to the skies.❞**
> **John Jones,** *The Cotton Mill*

1779	**1784**	**1796–7**
First iron bridge, over the River Severn, built in England	Henry Cort develops his puddling process for making wrought iron	Benyon, Bage and Marshall mill, Shrewsbury, England, constructed

Factory builders were soon adopting Darby's technology for their buildings. Calver Mill, Derbyshire, constructed in 1785, was the first to have floors supported by cast-iron columns; its beams were still made of timber. In 1792–3 successful factory-owner Richard Arkwright, in partnership with William Strutt, combined cast-iron columns with wooden beams covered in plaster to support floors made of brick arches. This breakthrough in design was claimed to be fireproof, and fireproof construction became the goal of factory builders from then on.

Smelting iron

The was a huge demand for iron during the industrial revolution, but a shortage of charcoal, the traditional material used to smelt the ore. Smelting with coal was possible, but sulphur in the coal made the resulting metal weak. Ironmaster Abraham Darby I found the solution to the problem in 1709 – roast the coal in an oven to remove the sulphur and produce coke. When used for smelting, coke had an advantage over charcoal, too: it was less inclined to crush, meaning that you could increase production by adding more coke and ore, and using larger blast furnaces. Coke-smelted cast iron was widely used for large building components, such as beams and columns, which could be cast to standard patterns in large quantities.

The final piece in the jigsaw was provided in 1796 at a mill at Shrewsbury. This mill, owned by three partners – Benyon, Bage and Marshall – had iron beams as well as iron columns, again supporting floors of brick. This building is the ancestor not only of countless iron-framed factories, but also, because of its use of a metal load-bearing frame, of the skyscrapers of the 20th century.

Wrought iron

Another major advance in iron production was the industrial production of the more malleable wrought iron. Ironmaster Henry Cort invented the process called puddling in 1784. This involved melting cast iron in a furnace and stirring it with a long pole, which had the effect of removing carbon from the metal. Wrought iron, which was more costly than cast iron, was not used widely for major structural components, such as columns, but was of great value in the production of building components, including ties, bolts and trusses, that had to be strong in tension.

The advantages of iron Mill owners quickly grasped the advantages of this type of structure. The fire risk was greatly reduced and the iron columns were slender and did not take up much floor space. The strong iron frame meant you could build more storeys because the structure no longer relied on the walls to bear its weight. And you could reduce the structure's weight further, enabling greater heights, by using hollow brick tiles for the floor arches rather than solid ones. Further refinements possible using cast-iron frames included passing steam through hollow columns to heat the building.

The iron-frame structure became the hallmark of industrial architecture. Factories and warehouses proliferated and these buildings, with their regular rows of windows echoing the regular grid of columns inside, became common in industrial towns and dockyards in many places in Europe and North America. Industry had found its expression in the built environment.

the condensed idea
Iron frames make fireproof factories

09 Taste

Today the term 'taste' is often used vaguely to mean personal preference or ephemeral fashion. But in the 18th century the term was employed in a much more focused way to indicate the specific qualities, artistic and moral, that led both to virtuous actions and good design. It was a powerful concept, and those who wielded it too enjoyed considerable power.

'"Beauty is truth, truth beauty," – that is all Ye know on earth, and all ye need to know.' Thus ends Keats's 'Ode on a Grecian Urn', one of the most famous poems in English. Written in the early 19th century, the poem's conclusion seems alien today, but in Keats's time the equation of truth and beauty would have seemed less peculiar because they harked back to the previous century, and a set of ideas that was hugely influential on artists and thinkers. These ideas concerned the concept of taste.

Shaftesbury and beauty The writer who first clearly defined the equation of truth with beauty was Anthony Ashley Cooper, third Earl of Shaftesbury. A member of the political classes, Shaftesbury was prevented by his health from continuing in politics so in his early thirties he turned to philosophy.

Unlike earlier philosophers, such as Thomas Hobbes, who saw mankind as pre-eminently selfish, Shaftesbury saw much more potential for virtue, for distinguishing between right and wrong, in humanity. Shaftesbury was also interested in aesthetics, the philosophy

timeline
1711

The Earl of Shaftesbury publishes *Characteristics of Men, Manners, Opinions, and Times,* collecting together some of his earlier philosophical writings

of the arts, and drew parallels between artistic beauty and virtue. The most radiant beauty for Shaftesbury was moral beauty, honesty, truth; but the converse for the philosophical earl was also true: artistic beauty was also morally good. As Keats would later, he equated beauty with truth, adding that beautiful architecture had true proportions.

Taste was the ability to be able to distinguish beauty from ugliness – and also to differentiate between moral good and bad. Taste was, therefore, a crucial business, and a person who had taste was an arbiter who would be listened to with care and seriousness. Such men were often referred to as virtuosi or connoisseurs. They were expected to have all the knowledge of artistic matters that these terms imply, and to be moral arbiters, too.

The rule of taste In the 18th century, most people believed that taste was something you were born with – anyone could read about it and understand it, but there were certain people, men of taste, who had the quality and who were marked as moral and aesthetic leaders. 18th-century writers talked about 'the rule of taste' – and arbiters of taste were expected to lay down the law on the subject.

The idea that true taste could not be taught was an attractive one to aristocrats and others in privileged positions with an interest in the arts.

> **For all Beauty is Truth. True Features make the Beauty of a face; and true Proportions the Beauty of Architecture; as true measures that of Harmony and Musick.**
> **Lord Shaftesbury**

1712
Shaftesbury addresses his *Letter concerning the Art or Science of Design* to Lord Somers

1719
Jonathan Richardson publishes his *Discourse on the Dignity, Certainty, Pleasure and Advantage of the Science of the Connoisseur*

1720
Lord Burlington practises as an architect, with the architect Henry Flitcroft acting as his assistant and draftsman

Decorum

The idea of decorum was used widely by writers about the arts, and usually indicated appropriateness – choice of the appropriate style, the appropriate proportions, the appropriate ornament and so on. Under the rule of taste, the ornamental excess of the baroque style and its use of deliberately distorted proportions was seen as indecorous; the more measured and harmonious style of Palladio, as in Dean Aldrich's work in Oxford (below), as the incarnation of decorum. In gardening, on the other hand, the rigorous symmetry of classicism was swept aside in favour of the less-formal landscape garden (see pages 44–47), and this was seen as decorous because it was appropriate for gardeners to work with the curves and irregularities of nature.

It meant, for example, that men such as the Earl of Burlington and Henry Aldrich, Dean of Christ Church, Oxford, had the confidence to become amateur architects and became highly influential when buildings were put up to their designs.

Those designs were classical. If true, harmonious proportions produced beauty in architecture, the architects of the 18th century saw this harmony most of all in the classical architecture of the great Palladio and his followers. So they left behind the ornate and complex architecture of the baroque, with all its curves and curlicues, and turned to the chaster Palladian style, which achieved its effects through proportion and adherence to classical rules. The clear value placed on this type of harmony by Shaftesbury and others was a vital element in the 18th-century Palladian revival (see page 23).

Burlington, rich, powerful and convinced of his role as arbiter of taste, was the most influential of the amateur Palladians, and his work won much admiration from aristocrats generally. Aldrich, who designed buildings for his Oxford college, Christ Church, with the first-ever 'palace front' in the Palladian style, was influential in church and university circles. The rule of taste pervaded the establishment.

A different taste Horace Walpole, the disciple of Gothic architecture, was well aware of this, and perhaps happy to subvert the idea when he transformed his Twickenham house, Strawberry Hill, in mock-medieval style. Rather than employing an architect to carry out the job, he did the design himself, in collaboration with a small group of friends and associates, whom he termed his 'Committee of Taste'. Such a name would have been seen as a joke on serious classicists and Palladians.

As architecture began to become more of a profession and less open to interested amateurs, taste became less important than a proper training in the basics of design and construction. But even among the professionals the idea that a true architecture is also the most beautiful held on through the 19th century, when the builders of Gothic churches declared that this style of building, as well as being admirable visually, was the most appropriate for Christianity and holiness.

the condensed idea
Good people produce good design

10 ROCOCO

Towards the end of the baroque period architects and, especially, interior designers turned away from the grandiose effects that sometimes dominated baroque architecture and produced a style with an altogether lighter touch, drawing especially on natural motifs, pale colours and gilding. This is the style known today as rococo, a style that has had a huge impact not just on architecture, but also on the design of all types of items from furniture to ceramics.

In some histories of architecture rococo is treated as a final stage of the baroque, while others see it as a style in its own right. Its distinctive features are the widespread use of S-shaped and C-shaped curves, often used very freely and loosely; generous applications of gilding; bright colours set against a pale or white background; and motifs drawn from nature, such as bunches of flowers, garlands of fruit and shells. As a rule symmetry, which had been a watchword in both classical and baroque design, was less important, and asymmetrical effects were taken up with enthusiasm.

Rococo interiors The rococo began as a French style. Painters, sculptors and interior decorators in France took it up from around 1690. It was seen first in the work of French designer Pierre Le Pautre, who worked for the architect Hardouin Mansart at several royal palaces, and popularized in a fashion for asymmetrically woven textiles, whose off-beat patterns have earned them the name 'bizarre silks'.

timeline

1730s	1745	1747
Rococo develops in France under the influence of painters such as Watteau and Boucher	Sans Souci Palace, Potsdam, Germany, begun to designs by Georg Wenzeslaus von Knobelsdorff	Queluz National Palace, Portugal, begun under architect Mateus Vicente de Oliveira

Stucco

Stucco is a type of plaster traditionally made of a mixture of sand, lime and water. It was widely used in both baroque and rococo – indoors and out – as a smooth, durable and weatherproof wall covering and as a means of decoration (below). Its decorative potential was much appreciated by baroque and rococo artists, who valued it because it could be applied to create smooth curves – ideal for creating the fluid spaces of 18th-century buildings – and for its sculptural quality. In rococo interiors where a *trompe l'oeil* effect was required, stucco could be used to create sculptures or reliefs of figures such as putti in a ceiling or flowers or fruit apparently growing up a wall. It was thus an ideal material for creating the types of illusions that rococo designers held so dear.

1752	1753	c.1760	1764
Catherine Palace, Tsarskoye Selo, Russia, rebuilt by Bartolomeo Rastrelli	William Hogarth's *Analysis of Beauty* mentions devices such as S-curves as being of the essence of beauty	William Chambers designs buildings for Kew Gardens, London, including a Chinese pagoda	Schloss Solitude, Germany, begun under the direction of Philippe de la Guêpière

> **'Thus it has happened . . . we must all seek the barbarous gaudy *goût* of the Chinese; and fat-headed Pagods and shaking Mandarins bear the prize from the greatest works of antiquity...'**
>
> **Mrs Elizabeth Montagu,** letter of 1749

After about 1730 the rococo started to spread beyond France, as patrons and designers alike began to appreciate the more delicate style of the Louis XV period. Fabrics and engraved illustrations took it deep into Germany and Central Europe, where it influenced the decoration of diverse buildings. The great churches of Bavaria, in which curvaceous baroque space is combined with delicate rococo painting and gilding, are one result of this visual traffic. Some of the rooms in Czech castles and palaces, such as the Masquerade Hall in the castle of Cesky Krumlov, its walls covered with *trompe l'oeil* masked figures, are another. Other Central European interiors evoke pastoral settings – country views, shepherds and farm scenes – in keeping with the fashion for pastoral in poetry and for aristocrats attempting to go back to nature by dressing up as shepherds.

Chinoiserie The 18th-century vogue for all things Chinese (see pages 60–63) was also at least in part influenced by the rococo movement. Like the rococo itself, the European interpretation of Chinese decoration was exotic, delicate and curvaceous. It was also far from authentic. European designers did not reproduce Chinese porcelain, furniture or buildings, they created their own versions of them, versions that were increasingly fanciful and remote from the originals. Motifs such as dragons, Chinese landscapes and people dressed in the Western idea of Chinese costume were all popular and sat comfortably beside other rococo elements.

Rococo façades Rococo also travelled to Russia, where its ideas influenced building exteriors as well as interiors, as a result of the imperial family looking to France and Italy for a dose of sophisticated and up-to-date culture. A notable example of this is the Catherine Palace in Tsarskoye Selo. The long façades of this vast imperial summer palace of the mid-18th century glisten with pale stucco and rich goldwork. It was the brainchild of Italian-born Francesco Bartolomeo Rastrelli, who was also the principal architect of the St Petersburg Winter Palace and numerous other Russian palaces in baroque and rococo styles.

An ephemeral style In other places, such as Britain, rococo did not take a firm hold, but had an influence on certain aspects of architecture and design, from the ornate furniture of Thomas Chippendale to the creations of the developing porcelain industry. Interiors and buildings decorated in the Chinese taste – delicate and exotic like the rococo – were also part of the general change in taste in the 18th century. But some of the best examples of British rococo decoration that were produced, including the structures in London pleasure gardens such as Vauxhall, have long since been demolished.

In most places rococo was a short-lived style, which took certain decorative trends in the baroque to extremes. It could often be whimsical, which suited the tastes and the pockets of aristocratic patrons who also had a taste for the filigree lightness of the early Gothic revival and for the type of architecture promoted by the later picturesque movement. In the long run, however, it was not so much these movements that replaced it as the coming fashion for neoclassicism.

the condensed idea
Flowers, fruit, scrolls and shells – delicacy in decoration

11 Genius loci

A new way of looking at gardening was pioneered by British landscape gardeners with their more 'natural' approach and promoted by poet Alexander Pope in the 18th century. The idea of gardens and buildings that respect nature and the spirit of the place continues to be influential on the way we think about the countryside, landscapes and places generally.

The idea that a place has a guardian spirit, a supernatural being that protects it, and that people visiting the place or living there must respect or worship it, goes back to the earliest forms of religion. In local belief systems from Japan to Africa, spirits of the place, deities of mountains and waterfalls, forests and trees, abound.

Local deities Respect for the local deity took different forms according to the place and culture – travellers might be expected to make an offering to the deity of the region they were passing through; and if they behaved disrespectfully they could expect the spirit to take revenge on them by making difficulties in their journey, or worse. The link between place and spirit could be very powerful.

The people who gave us our most familiar phrase for a spirit of place were the Romans, for whom the words *genius loci* meant the deity of a specific place – a locality or a specific feature of the topography, such as a volcano, a mountain or a notable tree. It was the Roman use of this term that was picked up by writers in the 18th century and which had a major effect on taste in Britain and beyond.

1731

Pope's Epistle IV to
Richard Boyle, Earl of
Burlington published

1741

Lancelot 'Capability' Brown is appointed
gardener at Stowe and makes the
garden more 'naturalistic' in style

Pope and the gardeners Alexander Pope was the most celebrated writer to use the phrase. Pope, writing principally about landscape gardening, but also applying his words to architecture, was reacting against the very formal tradition in gardening in the previous century, an era in which men such as the great French gardener André Le Nôtre created highly formal gardens, such as his masterpiece at Versailles. For Pope and the landscape gardeners of the 18th century, such complex gardens, patterned like intricate carpets, went against nature. They sought for a style of gardening that was more in tune with the surrounding landscape.

Pope's 'Epistle IV. To Richard Boyle, Earl of Burlington' stresses the importance of respecting nature and the spirit of the place whenever a person puts up a building or plans a landscape garden. The poet is particularly interested in landscape gardening in this poem and admires the way the great landscape gardeners used their skill to blend the garden with the surrounding landscape. But he also applies his ideas to architecture, instructing Burlington when 'To build, to plant, whatever you intend', to consider Nature.

> **Consult the Genius of the Place in all;**
> **That tells the Waters or to rise, or fall,**
> **Or helps th' ambitious Hill the heav'n to scale,**
> **Or scoops in circling theatres the Vale,**
> **Calls in the Country, catches opening glades,**
> **Joins willing woods, and varies shades from shades,**
> **Now breaks or now directs, th' intending Lines;**
> **Paints as you plant, and, as you work, designs.**

Alexander Pope

1741	**1764**	**1764**
Henry Hoare begins to design his outstanding landscape garden at Stourhead, Wiltshire	Brown begins work on the great garden at Blenheim Palace, Oxfordshire	Brown is appointed surveyor to the gardens of King George III

The landscape gardening movement As Pope describes, the Genius of the Place, then, controls the features of the landscape, and continues to control the effect of a scene as the gardener modifies it. The gardener has to work with it, rather than against it, and if this is done, can hope for satisfaction. This idea encouraged the landscape gardeners of the 18th and 19th centuries – such as Charles Bridgman and Lancelot 'Capability' Brown – to create the great 'naturalistic'

garden buildings

For hundreds of years people incorporated buildings into their gardens – to offer comfortable places to view the scenery or to give shelter from the rain. But the landscape gardens of the 18th century included more of these structures than ever before – a mass of gazebos, temples, umbrellos, rotundas and other structures. Many of these act as focal points, to lead the eye to a specific place in the garden and to create a particular atmosphere.

Landscape gardeners used temples like the one at Stourhead, below, to simulate 'Arcadian' valleys, and sham ruins to evoke the Gothic past. They could also use these buildings to express philosophical ideas. At the great English garden at Stowe, for example, Lord Cobham and his heirs erected symbolic buildings – such as a Temple of Ancient Virtues and a Temple of British Worthies – to express their philosophical and political views.

**‘Born to grace Nature and her works complete
With all that's beautiful, sublime and great!
For him each muse enwreathes the laurel crown
And consecrates to fame immortal Brown.’**

Anon, published by Horace Walpole, 1767

gardens that still surround many country houses. Painting with a broad brush, planting swathes of trees and digging long, sinuous lakes, they tried to work with nature. And architecture played its role in this approach, with garden buildings and houses placed with apparent casualness in these artificial landscapes.

This apparent insouciance was of course achieved with meticulous planning and hard work – sometimes whole villages were moved to accommodate these artificial landscapes. But the effect was to create buildings and spaces that were at one with nature and with the *genius loci*.

Although the era of the great landscape gardens and country houses is long gone, the notion of the *genius loci* has remained influential. The idea lies behind planning laws that restrict industrial developments in rural areas or high-rise building in country villages and towns. And it influences our sensibility when we praise the appearance of canals or railway lines of the 19th century, which follow contour lines and thus seem in part to respect nature, over roads, which often do not. It also influences the ideas of 'neo-rationalist' architects, such as the Italian Aldo Rossi, who design buildings in a style that draws much from traditional and vernacular architecture. And it informs the ideas of all who appreciate what is locally distinctive about particular towns and regions. From psychogeographers to conservationists, the *genius loci* is still a powerful spirit.

the condensed idea
The power of place

12 The picturesque

The picturesque movement began in England at the end of the 18th century as a reaction against the artificiality of British landscape gardens and the rigid symmetry of Palladian architecture. It changed the way people looked at both gardens and buildings, ushering in an appreciation of rustic cottages, ruins and the informal architecture of villas.

Towards the end of the 18th century, in England especially, people became more and more interested in the relationship between the house and garden. In the early part of the century this interest had resulted in the landscape gardening movement, in which gardeners such as 'Capability' Brown had laid out large gardens in great informal gestures, flooding valleys with lakes, planting groves of trees and setting pavilions and temples in the landscape to catch and delight the eye.

Questioning 'improvement' The landscape garden was a reaction to the highly formal gardens of the previous era. But the landscape garden itself was still artificial, still highly contrived, and their owners spoke endlessly of how they had 'improved' the landscape settings of their houses. In the 1780s and 1790s a reaction against this kind of 'improvement' on nature set in.

It was, to begin with, a literary reaction. Poets such as William Cowper saw the contradiction in improving on nature. Cowper put the boot firmly into Brown: 'Lo! He comes, – The omnipotent magician, Brown, appears . . . He speaks. The lake in front becomes a lawn, Woods vanish, hills subside, and vallies rise . . . ' Nature, unimproved, argued

timeline

1774	1792	1794
Downton Castle, Herefordshire, is built by Richard Payne Knight. It is a forerunner of Nash's castellated country houses	William Gilpin's *Three Essays: On Picturesque Beauty; On Picturesque Travel; and on Sketching Landscape* define the picturesque in these contexts	Publication of Richard Payne Knight's *The Landscape, A Didactic Poem* and Uvedale Price's *Essay on the Picturesque*

The cottage orné

The interest in the picturesque landscape made people see country buildings, especially cottages, in a new way – for the first time they were widely seen as objects for aesthetic appreciation. As a result, Nash and other architects of the period developed the *cottage orné*, or ornamental cottage, which exemplified picturesque ideals. The typical *cottage orné* was asymmetrical, thatched and had dormer windows in the roof. It often had a veranda or porch with a roof held up by rustic posts. Many landowners built such cottages on their estates – some even built big versions for themselves or their families. Such buildings still influence our ideals of 'quaint' or picturesque country cottages today.

Cowper, was better than this, because it had been made by God, and it was presumptuous of would-be magicians to alter it.

New views of landscape More books followed, echoing this attack – but also adapting it to make room for a new kind of landscape and architecture, which people called the picturesque. As its name suggests, its key idea was that landscape should resemble the beauty found in painting – especially the great landscape paintings of the 17th century. An important contributor to the debate about the picturesque was the vicar and travel-writer William Gilpin. But three publications by others were especially influential. The first, *The Landscape, a Didactic Poem* (1794), was by Richard Payne Knight, an English country gentleman who attacked the artificiality of Brown's work.

1795	**c.1802**	**1808**	**1812**
Publication of Humphry Repton's *Sketches and Hints on Landscape Gardening*	John Nash designs Cronkhill, Shropshire, an asymmetrical Italianate villa	Carhayes Castle, Cornwall, by John Nash, a castellated Gothic house with round towers, is one of several in this style by Nash	John Nash designs Blaise Hamlet, a group of cottages ornés near Bristol

❝. . . in new creations the architect considers the house . . . and the plantations as a great whole.❞

J.B. Papworth, *Hints on Ornamental Gardening*

The same year saw the publication of the long *Essay of the Picturesque* by Sir Uvedale Price, a friend of Knight. In his book, Price extended the idea philosophically. He saw the picturesque as an aesthetic quality that he distinguished from two other influential concepts, the sublime and the beautiful, which the philosopher Edmund Burke had defined. Price's essay also covers more practical areas, recommending that gardeners study the works of the greatest landscape painters, especially Salvator Rosa. The great French landscape masters Claude and Poussin were also favourite painters of disciples of the picturesque.

Still more practical was Humphry Repton's *Sketches and Hints on Landscape Gardening*. Repton was a working landscape gardener, and no doubt hoped to promote his own practice with his book. He was certainly successful – he was already the leading garden designer of the age when his book was published – and he transformed many gardens along picturesque lines in the years either side of 1800.

Architecture and the picturesque The picturesque ideal was not only about gardening. It had a big influence on architecture, too. For much of the 18th century the classical symmetry of the Palladian style had dominated English architecture. Now architecture began to relish asymmetry. Villas appeared with a round tower at one corner, with an offset doorway or some other feature that defied the rigid proportions of Palladianism. There was also a new interest in the cottage as a building worthy of serious architectural thinking.

The most successful architect of the picturesque was John Nash. He began to design asymmetrical Italianate 'villas' with corner towers, and was also interested in the way in which Gothic architecture could fit into the picturesque landscape. Other architects followed, and there was

castles and ruins

Followers of the picturesque liked ruins and prized landscapes in which ancient abbeys or castles appeared as intricate visual punctuation on hill tops or in valley bottoms. It was not long before gardeners began to build new ruins as landscape eyecatchers. Such buildings, apparently purposeless, are nowadays often referred to as follies. But originally many doubled as workers' houses, shelters for those strolling through the garden or prospect towers from which one could admire the view.

a widespread freeing-up of domestic architecture in Britain, with less symmetry and formality. It was a mood that seemed to suit the atmosphere of the Regency and the unbuttoned, not to say extravagant, character of the Prince Regent himself.

The wider impact The picturesque movement was mirrored by similar ideas in other countries, including France, where the influence of Jean-Jacques Rousseau – who argued that humankind was essentially innocent, but had been corrupted by the life of the city – was strong. And the picturesque movement, with its emphasis on the natural, was a key influence on Romanticism, the cultural movement that was sweeping Europe at this time. Its importance thus goes far beyond the gardens and houses where it began.

the condensed idea
Pictorial values
meet architecture

13 Neoclassicism

In the last few decades of the 18th century a new attitude to the ancient remains of Greece and Rome began to emerge. Archaeologists and architects began to record these buildings more meticulously, making and publishing measured drawings that had a huge influence, bringing a new type of classicism into fashion in Britain, France and America.

The influence of Andrea Palladio transformed the architecture of Europe, bringing classical architecture to places such as Britain (see pages 20–23). But Palladianism was a very particular type of classical architecture, based on the ideas of a 16th-century Italian rather than on the buildings of the ancient world. In the mid 18th century a group of architects began to look further back in time for their inspiration in a bid to create architecture based not on the buildings of the Renaissance, but on those of antiquity – ancient Rome and ancient Greece.

Buried cities unearthed They were helped in this by the rise of a new discipline, archaeology. In the 1730s and 1740s people saw some of the most dramatic of all archaeological revelations – the lost Roman cities of Pompeii and Herculaneum, buried beneath the volcanic debris of Vesuvius, began to be unburied.

Suddenly, modern scholars and artists were closer than ever before to the Romans themselves because the excavations famously revealed not just buildings, but also the actual people, the petrified imprints of their bodies as if frozen in time. In addition, importantly for architecture and the decorative arts, remains of wall paintings, furniture and other domestic

timeline

1748	1753	1760–70	1761–4
Excavations begin at Pompeii	Robert Wood's *Ruins of Palmyra*	Robert Adam designs the interiors at Kedleston Hall, Derbyshire	Ange-Jacques Gabriel designs the Petit Trianon at Versailles for Louis XV

items brought people closer than ever to the way the Romans arranged and adorned their homes. The quality and number of discoveries stunned the world.

Recording antiquity Meanwhile two British architects, James Stuart and Nicholas Revett, spent three years in Athens in the early 1750s measuring and drawing many of the ancient buildings. They took the fruits of their work back to England in 1755 and, after a long delay during which Stuart bought Revett's interest in the drawings, the first volume of *The Antiquities of Athens* was published in 1762. Three further volumes appeared over the following decades, the last in 1816. The work of Stuart and Revett was but a major part of a wider movement. Several volumes on Roman antiquities, including Charles-Louis Clérisseau's *Antiquities of Nîmes* (1778), also appeared.

Although neither Stuart nor Revett designed many buildings, their publication made them famous, especially Stuart, who earned the nickname 'Athenian' Stuart. But one very active and successful

Etruscan style

Another influence on interior decoration in the late 18th century was the painted pottery unearthed in the ancient Greek world. Much of this was thought to be Etruscan, so the 18th-century decorative style using a similar palette of black, terracotta and white also became known as Etruscan. Pale, cameo-like figures on a darker ground were also used. Robert Adam was an exponent of the style, as was the Frenchman François-Joseph Bélanger. The famous Jasper Wares produced by the British potter Josiah Wedgwood were also influenced by this Etruscan style, and Wedgwood named his factory 'Etruria'.

1762	**1762–69**	**1764**	**1817**
James Stuart and Nicholas Revett, *The Antiquities of Athens*, volume one	Robert Adam remodels the interiors of Syon House, near London	Robert Adam, *Ruins of the Palace of the Emperor Diocletian at Spalato in Dalmatia*	Library of the University of Virginia, Charlottesville, built to earlier designs by Thomas Jefferson

> ❝...we flatter ourselves, we have been able to seize, with some degree of success, the beautiful spirit of antiquity, and to transfuse it with novelty and variety, through all our numerous works.❞
>
> Robert Adam, preface to
> *The Works in Architecture of Robert and James Adam Esquires*

architect followed in their footsteps, making and publishing accurate drawings of ancient buildings, the Scotsman Robert Adam. Adam travelled to Italy in search of Palladian inspiration, but he met Clérisseau and the two men travelled together to Split in Croatia to make measured drawings of the enormous palace of the emperor Diocletian. The drawings were published in 1764.

So during the second half of the 18th century, architects and clients, especially in Britain, became aware for the first time of the exact details and proportions of the buildings of ancient Greece. Their knowledge of the Roman world was also enhanced. This was true especially of Roman domestic buildings – hitherto temple architecture had been the main source for architects; with the excavations of Pompeii and Adam's work at Split much more was known about Roman houses and palaces.

Robert Adam This work had a huge impact on architecture. Adam's delicate style of interior decoration, for example, owes much to his studies of Roman wall-painting, but also draws on Greek motifs, such as vine patterns, and ideas about the artistic style of the Etruscans.

At Syon House in Middlesex, he even incorporated genuine ancient Roman marble columns, hauled out of the River Tiber, into one of the interiors. These stunning columns are adorned with capitals inspired by Greek architecture and topped with gilded statues of the type the Romans might have placed on a triumphal arch. Adam, though influenced by scholarship, was not afraid to mix up sources in order to create a dramatic effect.

Neoclassical motifs

A number of motifs were widely used by the architects and decorators of the 18th century and became closely identified with classicism. These include the interlocking 'Greek key' design (below), the palmette (a palm-leaf design) (right) and the anthemion (a plant motif similar to the flower of the honeysuckle). The palmette and anthemion often appear together, alternating in a frieze.

Neoclassical forms Adam's genius, so often called on to remodel country house interiors, brought out the decorative, filigree aspects of ancient architecture, the aspects that could be expressed in paint, plasterwork, gilding and the occasional marble column. Other architects drew more closely on the actual form of ancient Greek and Roman buildings. Thomas Jefferson, for example, designed the library of the University of Virginia at Charlottesville in the form of the Roman circular temple the Pantheon, a shape also adopted by the architect Georg von Knobelsdorff for the Catholic church of St Hedwig in Berlin. French architects, such as Etienne-Louis Boullée and Claude-Nicolas Ledoux, took neoclassicism in a different direction (see page 56–59), radically extending its forms.

the condensed idea
Architecture plus archeology

14 Reason

At the height of the Enlightenment, architects in France turned to an architecture that attempted to use pure forms, such as pyramids, cylinders and spheres, with a new rationality, as if applying the notion of reason to building. Their influence spread beyond the Age of Reason itself to inspire a very different generation of artists and thinkers.

For many, the 18th century was the Age of Reason and the time of the Enlightenment – the cultural movement that embodied free-thinking, scepticism and scientific thought. The thinkers of the Enlightenment looked back to the great rational scientists and philosophers of the 17th century, figures such as Descartes in France and Newton in England, and valued a combination of scientific understanding and free thought. They included writers such as Voltaire and Rousseau, and their watchwords were reason and rationalism.

From neoclassicism to pure geometry When the Enlightenment philosophers were flourishing, the prevailing architectural style was neoclassicism. In many ways it must have seemed an appropriate style, highly ordered, adaptable to virtually any type of building and not closely associated with the Christian religion, which some of the *philosophes* rejected. A classical library seemed an ideal setting for Enlightenment inquiry; a classical drawing room a perfect place for a philosophical discussion between colleagues or friends.

But there were some architects who wanted to take further the link between architecture and ideas. They aimed to create buildings that

timeline

1775	1784
Ledoux's Saltworks at Arc-et-Senans begun	Boullée publishes his design for a monument to Isaac Newton

were a three-dimensional embodiment of the geometry and mathematics that underlay the philosophical ideas of the Age of Reason, in the process thinking every structure through from first principles. These architects, Frenchmen Etienne-Louis Boullée and Claude-Nicholas Ledoux, produced buildings – or at least designs, since not all these projects were actually built – that resembled nothing seen before or since.

The Sublime

First explored in an anonymous ancient Greek text, *On the Sublime* (said to be by Longinus), the idea of the sublime became especially popular in the 18th century. The Sublime encompasses ideas of the awe inspired by vast phenomena (especially natural phenomena) and the strong emotions associated with religion. The idea was discussed by the British

philosopher Edmund Burke, analysed by the German Immanuel Kant, and influenced several art forms, especially literature (where it resided in the emotions engendered by wild scenery or the vastness of the cosmos) and painting (where it influenced both the imagery of landscape painting and of canvasses depicting supernatural subjects, such as ghosts). In architecture structures such as Boullée's Newton Monument (above), for all their rationality, show in their vast size the influence of thinking about the Sublime.

1784–7

A series of 50 gates or barriers are built around Paris to the designs of Ledoux

1788

Boullée's design for a Royal Library published

1804

Ledoux publishes his design for an Inspector's House at the source of the River Loüe and his 'ideal town of Chaux'

Boullée's geometrical forms The most shocking of these structures were designed by Boullée and his most famous design is a monument to one of the fathers of the Enlightenment, the British scientist Isaac Newton. Boullée's Newton monument was to be in the form of a hollow empty sphere 152 metres (500 ft) in diameter. The upper part was to be pierced with holes so that tiny pinpricks of light would shine through like stars. There was also to be a lamp suspended from the ceiling, to represent the sun. Boullée, in other words, was proposing a vast model of the universe to commemorate the person who had done most to explain how the cosmos works.

Not surprisingly, Boullée's vast Newton monument was never built. Neither was his royal library, with its terraces of books inside an enormous cylindrical shape. Nor were other structures he proposed in the form of outsize cones or pyramids. They remained on paper, as extraordinary workings-out of ways of using 'pure' forms to make unprecedented buildings.

Ledoux's *architecture parlante* Less outré than Boullée, and more successful at getting his projects built, was Claude-Nicholas Ledoux. He was the architect of a set of 50 toll gates around the edge of Paris (four of which still stand) and of the extraordinary Inspector's House at the source of the River Loüe, a structure designed in part as a cylinder through which the river gushes in a continuous waterfall. It is

Frozen Music

The great German Romantic writer Johann Wolfgang von Goethe produced one of the most memorable metaphors when he described architecture as 'frozen music'. The phrase suggests that buildings have the ability to inspire emotions and to grip the imagination, just as music does, but that they are also frozen in time. This resonant phrase points to both architecture's symbolic power and to its ability to overwhelm the beholder, in a way that is similar to the works of the French Enlightenment designers.

> **❛Ledoux refused to accept either Palladio or the Greeks. He . . . wanted to re-think the problem, and re-feel the character, of every job.❜**
>
> **Nikolaus Pevsner,** *An Outline of European Architecture*

hard to imagine a closer unity of purpose and structure, and the house illustrates Ledoux's notion of '*l'architecture parlante*', an architecture that speaks its purpose.

Ledoux's masterpiece is the Royal Saltworks at Arc-et-Senans near Besançon. The house for the Director of the Saltworks, its entrance portico dazzling with tall, rusticated coloumns, is a show-stopping building. But still more remarkable was the 'ideal town' of Chaux that Ledoux planned to complement the Saltworks. Around the works was an oval of houses for the workers, beyond this an array of public buildings: a catacomb in the shape of a vast sphere; the Pacifère, a building where disputes would be settled; temples of Memory and Virtue; and a Temple of Love planned in the shape of an erect penis.

Beyond reason For all their symbolism, though, these buildings go beyond rationality. Their very vastness, not to mention their sheer nerve, inspires awe in the beholder. So, as well as looking back at the Age of Reason, these designs also look forward to the fascination with powerful natural forces that characterized Romanticism, the cultural movement that emphasized the individual artist, and that took pleasure in contemplating the great spectacles of nature – from mountains to waterfalls – and the emotions they inspire in humankind.

the condensed idea
Pure forms embody ideas

15 Orientalism

Western Europe became fascinated with 'the Orient' in the late 17th and 18th centuries, as links with China and India became stronger. Few European architects had a deep understanding of oriental architecture, but many were inspired by the details of Chinese and Indian buildings, and used these details as motifs to create deliberately exotic and enticing designs.

For hundreds of years the great civilization of China was little known in the West, but during the 16th and 17th centuries, as Western travellers began to explore the globe, a few Europeans, most of them missionaries sent by the Catholic church, reached China and sent back accounts of the country. Some of these publications, notably the 17th-century *Embassy* by Dutchman Jan Nieuhof, included engravings of Chinese buildings.

The taste for 'the Orient' These publications fired the imagination of rulers and aristocrats, and one or two of them began to use Chinese elements in their buildings. One of the first was Louis XIV, who in the 1670s built a 'Trianon de Porcelaine' with a blue-and-white-tiled roof that does not survive.

The fashion for Chinese buildings caught on more widely in the 18th century, when Chinese porcelain began to be imported to Europe in larger quantities. No doubt a mixture of influences – old books, designs on porcelain, memories of earlier buildings such as Louis' short-lived Trianon – inspired the Prussian emperor Frederick II when he built his Chinese teahouse in the grounds of his Palace of Sans Souci, Potsdam.

timeline

1757	1757
Chinese teahouse, Palace of Sans Souci, Potsdam, is built for the emperor Frederick II	Sir William Chambers publishes *Designs of Chinese Buildings, Furniture, Dresses, Machines, and Utensils*

Pattern books

The 18th century was the great age of the architectural pattern book, a publication full of illustrations of examples of architectural details (and sometimes whole buildings), which builders could use to copy or adapt. Many pattern books contained pages of classical details, but some contained oriental motifs. One of the best known was William Halfpenny's *Rural Architecture in the Chinese Taste* (1750–2), which included designs for doors, gates, bridges and small buildings with pagoda-like roofs (right) and dragon ornaments. Other publications, including William and John Halfpenny's *Chinese and Gothic Architecture Properly Ornamented* (1752) and Matthew Darly's *A New Book of Chinese, Gothic and Modern Chairs* (c.1750), also spread the word.

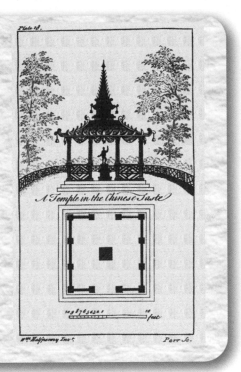

This structure of 1757, one of many pavilions in Frederick's lavish garden, is like no genuine Chinese building. But it has elements influenced by the Chinese taste – columns in the form of palm trees, a roof with slight curves and statues of Chinese figures mark this building out as oriental.

A spreading fashion During the next 50 or 60 years buildings like this, incorporating elements of oriental style, caught on widely across Europe. A pavilion at Drottningholm, Sweden, and the Palazzina la Favorita, Palermo, are two famous examples. But in aristocratic gardens

1769	1799	1805	1818–22
Pavilion at Drottningholm, Sweden, completed	Palazzina la Favorita, Palermo, constructed	Work on Sezincote, Gloucestershire, England, begun in the Indian Islamic style	Royal Pavilion, Brighton, built for the Prince Regent (the future King George IV)

up and down Europe, many smaller Chinese gazebos and pavilions appeared, and some more adventurous patrons even began to commission interior decoration in the Chinese taste.

Publications fuelled the fashion. Sir William Chambers was the greatest, and best informed, advocate of the Chinese style. Unlike any other British architect, Chambers had actually visited China, travelling there several times as a young man when he worked for the Swedish East India Company. In 1757 he published *Designs of Chinese Buildings, Furniture, Dresses, Machines, and Utensils*. The book contains engravings of various Chinese buildings, including houses, pavilions, bridges, temples and pagodas.

In Britain at this time, most architects looked down on oriental culture. To be a serious architect you were supposed to study classical buildings. But Chambers had the ear of the young Prince of Wales, soon to be crowned as King George III. Soon he was working on the remodelling of the royal gardens at Kew, and building a great pagoda there. The oriental taste was established. Pattern books illustrating garden buildings with upturned roofs, frilly looking decoration, dragon ornaments and fancy 'Chinese paling' fences, became popular.

Sharawaggi

This outlandish-looking word, which may come from the Japanese, was first used by a 17th-century writer, Sir William Temple, to describe the asymmetry and irregularity that was such a fetching feature of Chinese garden design. The word became fashionable in the 18th century, particularly when taken up by Horace Walpole, who praised 'the *Sharawaggi*, or Chinese want of symmetry, in buildings, as in grounds or gardens'. Walpole was an enthusiast for the Gothic style, but he liked the playfulness of line, the use of twists and turns, the general irregularity of Chinese design because they were the opposite of classicism. For many, oriental asymmetry was a liberation, and sharawaggi became a cult term of praise when talking about everything from ceramics to buildings.

❝ If you have a region of wilderness where you want to build some ethnic dwellings clothed in exotic garb, then the Chinese is sure to be most acceptable. ❞

Prince de Ligne, *adviser to Marie Antoinette*

Other oriental styles Thanks to Britain's imperial ambitions, Europe was also discovering the architecture of India. Indian and Chinese styles were frequently mixed and confused. People were apt to refer to pagodas as Indian, or to mistake Indian Islamic buildings for Hindu temples.

The confusion and combination of Chinese and Indian styles reached its peak in the Royal Pavilion at Brighton, the seaside palace designed for the Prince Regent by John Nash in 1818–22. From the outside this building is a confection of onion domes, minarets, openwork screens and other Indian details. It is heavily influenced by Indian Islamic buildings, but with Nash's own whimsical twist. Inside, however, the decoration is in the Chinese taste, with palm-tree columns and Chinese-wallpaper designs.

The exotic taste The bizarre combination of styles at Brighton is an extreme example, but it shows how European architects regarded oriental design. They saw the Chinese buildings drawn by Chambers and the Indian architecture described by merchants and officials as sources they could quarry to create an exotic impression. This could be especially effective in garden buildings, where appearance was all. And one or two larger structures, such as Frederick II's tea house, the Prince Regent's Brighton Pavilion or a country house such as Sezincote, also made effective use of the oriental mode.

the condensed idea
Chinese taste travels west

16 Restoration

For centuries when a building needed repairing, people replaced the defective fabric in the manner of the day, so that old buildings gradually turned into an amiable hotchpotch of styles. But in the late 18th century a new awareness of the history of medieval architecture plus a powerful religious revival combined to make architects think again. It became fashionable to replace old fabric in a style similar to what was built in the Middle Ages: restoration was born.

The idea of restoration had its heyday in the late 18th and 19th centuries. This was a period when many of Britain's medieval churches were in a sad state of disrepair, having survived centuries of change and decay. Transformed for Puritan worship in the 17th century (when stained-glass windows were removed and frescoes painted over with whitewash), many were then transformed again in the 18th century, the age of the sermon, with the addition of box pews and oversize pulpits. But the 18th century, as well as being the age of the sermon, was also, for many churches, the age of neglect, when buildings were run down, clerics were often absentees and roofs leaked.

A religious revival The Victorian period, by contrast, saw a religious revival. The Evangelical movement brought an emphasis on the Gospels, the Bible and personal religious experience. The very different Oxford movement stressed the importance of traditional liturgy and presented Anglicanism as a branch of Christianity on the same footing as the Catholic and Orthodox churches. Through these differing

timeline

1786
James Wyatt restores
Hereford Cathedral

1850s
George Gilbert Scott
restores Exeter Cathedral

An early reaction

Almost from the beginning, restoration had a bad name with those who were willing to think outside the religious box. The first recorded use of the word 'restoration' occurs in the long, mock-epic poem *Don Juan*, by Lord Byron. Canto XVI of the poem introduces us to an English aristocrat who (like the poet himself, whose home was Newstead Abbey in Nottinghamshire, below) lives in a building that was once an abbey. Lord Henry has had his grand home restored by an architect who was keen to do rather more than patch it up:

> There was a modern Goth, I mean a Gothic
> Bricklayer of Babel, called an architect,
> Brought to survey these grey walls, which though so thick,
> Might have from time acquired some slight defect;
> Who, after rummaging the Abbey through thick
> And thin, produced a plan whereby to erect
> New buildings of correctest conformation,
> And throw down old, which he called *restoration*.

Byron liked to make fun of what he called cant. He saw through the presumption of architects who talked about restoring buildings when they were actually building anew in a way that reflected some modern idea of what an old building should be like.

1857
Scott begins extensive restoration of Lichfield Cathedral

1862–70
Scott restores Ripon Cathedral

1871
G.E. Street begins his restoration of York Minster

1884–86
J.L. Pearson rebuilds tower of Peterborough Cathedral

agencies, religion was very much in the air, and church building and the proper maintenance of old churches became burning issues.

For most, under the influence of the Gothic revival (see page 68), 'proper maintenance' meant the use of the Gothic style. And this maintenance was seen as a chance to restore churches to an imagined former medieval glory. Yet it was impossible to know exactly what church buildings had looked like 600 years earlier – the process always involved guesswork.

Restoring and 'improving' One example of this process was the restoration of Hereford Cathedral undertaken by James Wyatt after the medieval west tower collapsed in 1786. This was a building that had evolved over the centuries, with parts in the round-arched style of the Normans, other parts in the pointed-arched Gothic style that followed it. Wyatt saw the restoration as a chance to sweep away the Norman round arches and replace them with 'correct' and consistent pointed ones. When he had finished, the building seemed thoroughly Gothic.

Sir George Gilbert Scott

Scott was one of the most successful of all Victorian architects. In a career spanning more than 40 years he produced such important structures as the government offices in London's Whitehall, the chapel of Exeter College, Oxford, and the Albert Memorial, Kensington Gardens, London. His practice was so large and widespread, and his activity so relentless, that he sometimes forgot which job he was on. Scott restored several cathedrals, including Chester, Chichester, Ely, Exeter, Lichfield, Ripon and Salisbury – undoing some of Wyatt's poor work at the latter. His touch was usually more gentle than that of Wyatt, but he was still much more inclined to rebuild than a modern conservationist would be.

> **❝. . . the spirit of the dead workman cannot be summoned up, and commanded to direct other hands, and other thoughts. And as for direct and simple copying, it is palpably impossible. What copying can there be of surfaces that have been worn half an inch down?❞**

John Ruskin, *The Seven Lamps of Architecture*

Wyatt did similar things at other cathedrals, where 'inconsistent' features, such as a free-standing bell tower at Salisbury, were removed. Later Gothic architects, such as Sir George Gilbert Scott and George Edmund Street, restored hundreds of churches, although often with a gentler hand than Wyatt had displayed.

In France, too, architects such as Viollet-le-Duc (see page 70) chiselled their way through churches and châteaux. Viollet, in particular, was keen to make buildings better, somehow more authentic, by adding 'correct' features to make them look more medieval.

So 'restoration' could mean much more than putting back old features and mending holes in roofs. It could amount to a virtual rebuilding in the architect's or incumbent's idea of the ideal Gothic style and it frequently involved 'replacing' features so worn away that the restorer could have little idea what they originally looked like. It was a con, essentially, albeit a con often undertaken for the best of reasons, with religious sanction and sometimes with stunning architectural results. And yet we owe something to the restorers, too, for they did save many buildings that might, without their too-eager attentions, have collapsed into rubble like the western tower at Hereford.

the condensed idea
The repairer knows best

17 Revivalism

The Victorian period was the heyday of revivalist architecture, a way of building in which style was a question of reproducing the architecture of the past. The most popular and persistent form of revivalism was the Gothic revival, the imitation of the pointed-arched styles of the medieval churches. The Gothic revival swept across towns and cities because the style was used to build not only churches, but also town halls, schools, railway stations, even factories and warehouses.

In the 19th century Gothic architecture – pointed-arched and stone-built, according to the structural and visual logic of the Middle Ages – made a major comeback. Credit for reviving this more 'correct' kind of Gothic goes largely to two architects – Englishman Augustus Welby Northmore Pugin and Frenchman Eugène-Emmanuel Viollet-le-Duc. They looked at Gothic very differently, but their combined influence was enormous.

The work of Pugin A.W.N. Pugin was a Catholic and is best known today for his work (with Charles Barry) on the Houses of Parliament in London. In 1836 he began a one-man campaign to reform English architecture. Pugin's big idea was that Gothic represented a culture – medieval Christian civilization – that was far preferable to that of his own time. So in 1836 he published a book with a title that summed up his argument: *Contrasts; or, A Parallel Between the Noble Edifices of the Fourteenth and Fifteenth Centuries, and Similar Buildings of the Present Day; Shewing the Present-Day Decay of Taste.*

timeline

1833	1836	1846	1846
Oxford Movement founded	A.W.N. Pugin's *Contrasts* published	Pugin's St Giles's, Cheadle, completed	Richard Upjohn's Trinity Church, New York City, completed

In *Contrasts* illustrations of idealized medieval towns were set next to images of the industrial and architectural squalor of the 19th century. A Victorian poor-house, a building resembling a prison, was contrasted, for example, with a medieval monastery, where comfort and charity were given to the poor. Pugin followed up *Contrasts* with another book, *The True Principles of Pointed or Christian Architecture* (1841). Together,

The Ecclesiology movement

In the 1830s a number of Oxford-based theologians began to speak out loudly against what they saw to be two threats to the Anglican church – the rise of liberalism and the developments in science that challenged such orthodoxies as the account of the creation in the Bible. They published a series of tracts about their ideas (this led to the movement's alternative name, Tractarianism) and argued for a church with spirituality and ritual at its centre. A parallel movement in Cambridge, known at first as the Cambridge Camden Society and later as the Ecclesiological Society entered the area of architecture head-on, with a series of pamphlets containing clear instructions for church-building. In particular, they recommended that nave and chancel should be clearly separated, with the chancel more highly ornamented than the nave, to enable a proper focus on the high altar. There should also be a vestry for the priest and a porch at the church entrance. Georgian features, such as galleries, were frowned on and Gothic was the style of choice. These recommendations for the Anglican church were very similar to Pugin's for Catholic churches and together both had a strong influence on the way new churches were built and old churches were restored.

1851–53	1863	1867	1889
John Ruskin, *Stones of Venice*, promotes Venetian Gothic	E.-E. Viollet-le-Duc, *Entretiens sur l'Architecture* first volume published	Sir Charles Barry and Pugin's Houses of Parliament, London, completed	James Renwick's St Patrick's Cathedral, New York City, completed

these works set out his big idea: that we should revive Gothic – and, preferably, Catholicism – and improve our social, moral and architectural lot.

Pugin designed stunning Gothic churches decorated and fitted out in the manner of medieval examples. At their best, as at St Giles, Cheadle, they glow like jewel-boxes with wall paintings and stained glass. Even Anglicans were impressed. And at the same time the Anglican Church (and its North American counterpart, the Episcopalian) began to make a parallel, if partial, return to medieval values and aesthetics. This happened under the auspices of the Ecclesiological movement, which sought to return Anglican churches to something like their medieval Gothic splendour. British writer John Ruskin, another enthusiastic promoter of Gothic, also had a strong influence on the spread of the style.

Viollet-le-Duc Meanwhile in France, another great writer-architect, Viollet-le-Duc, was campaigning on behalf of a revival of Gothic. His most influential work was *Entretiens sur l'Architecture* (Discourses on

Other revivals

Although Gothic (right) was the most widely revived style in the 19th century, other past styles were reinvented, too. Some saw the round-arched Romanesque style of the early Middle Ages as appropriate as Gothic for churches. It was revived in Britain and Germany, where it became known as the *Rundbogenstil* (round-arched style). Large country houses were built in every style from Gothic to classical, but a style imitating the heavy forms of Scottish medieval architecture became popular as the baronial style. Later in the century there was a Tudor revival, often incorporating timber-framed gables, that became known as Old English. All these revivals were stimulated by a raft of scholarship about the architecture of the past, published in books lavishly illustrated with engravings.

ST. GILES', CHEADLE.

> **On comparing the Architectural Works of the present Century with those of the Middle Ages, the wonderful superiority of the latter must strike every attentive observer.**
>
> A.W.N. Pugin, *Contrasts*

Architecture), which came out in two volumes in 1863–72. Viollet's emphasis was different from that of Pugin. His great idea was that the Gothic form of structure – with piers, ribbed vaults and buttresses – was a supremely logical way to build that could be adapted with modern materials, such as cast iron.

The result, in mainland Europe, Britain and North America, was a concerted revival of the Gothic style. It was used widely to build new churches for the expanding population, to restore old churches and to build all types of structures, from law courts to railway stations. Major architects embraced Gothic, and this major artistic revival transformed cities from Philadelphia to Paris.

A varied revival The buildings these architects produced were hugely varied. While some preferred the ornate Gothic of the 14th century in England, others went for an earlier, plainer version of the style as it first began in 13th-century France. Some were influenced by the Gothic of Venice, which had been vigorously praised by Ruskin. Yet others took the style in intriguing new directions unthought-of by any medieval mason. But whichever type of Gothic they chose, the spires of their churches and the pinnacles attached to their town halls and warehouses transformed city skylines and country landscapes alike.

the condensed idea
Gothic is the answer to our troubles

18 Prefabrication

Working on site is a slow, complex and messy business. But there is another way to build that avoids some of the complexity and mess – assembling a building from a kit of parts prepared beforehand. This type of building works in a different way from traditional building, and it has proved hugely successful in certain types of structure, especially industrial buildings, since Victorian times.

People tried applying the idea of prefabrication to building as long ago as the Middle Ages, assembling timber-framed houses by constructing parts of the frame in the carpenter's workshop and then carrying them to the site where they were 'raised' into position.

These early prefabricated houses were a success, but each frame was custom-made, every building was unique. The big step in prefabrication, the step that really cut down the labour and made building a matter of assembling parts, was to make the parts interchangeable. This step was first taken in the 19th century, when the labour-saving machines of the industrial revolution could make building still faster and more standardized. The greatest advocate of this way of building was the British gardener and designer Joseph Paxton.

The great greenhouses Joseph Paxton worked at the Royal Botanic Gardens at Kew before going to Chatsworth to become the head gardener on the Duke of Devonshire's estate. While at Chatsworth, Paxton developed his flair as a designer of greenhouses,

timeline

1836

Joseph Paxton begins work on the Great Stove, the pioneering greenhouse at Chatsworth, Derbyshire

noting that the existing houses, with their thick glass and heavy timberwork, were gloomy inside. So he began to develop new glasshouse structures with thin glazing bars, wooden frames and columns made of cast iron. His Lily House – almost 30 metres (100 ft) in length – and his Great Stove (1836–40), an enormous hothouse, were two of his triumphs.

New technologies In the course of this work, Paxton realized that he could stretch existing technology. For example, he was impressed by the work of Robert Chance, a glass manufacturer who had improved the cylinder glass-making technique so that he could produce sheets of glass

The 'prefab'

In the 1930s a number of architects, including Walter Gropius, designed mass housing made of factory-produced components and assembled on site. A concerted effort to make this type of housing came about in Britain after the Second World War, when a shortage of housing and surplus capacity in factories that had been producing military aircraft were key factors.

'Prefabs' were intended to be made in these spare factories and assembled as temporary housing that would last between 10 and 15 years. Several thousand of these mainly aluminium- or asbestos-cement-walled bungalows were built, and they proved popular with residents, who liked their modern fittings and pleasant, light interiors. In many cases these 'prefabs' lasted several decades and a few still survive (right).

1850	1851	1944
Walter Macfarlane of Glasgow publishes his first catalogue of prefabricated buildings	Great Exhibition opens at the Crystal Palace, Hyde Park, London	British Temporary Housing Programme, with prefabricated bungalows, launched

nearly 1 metre (3 ft) in length. He pressed Chance: if the glazier could make sheets 1.2 metres (4 ft) long, Paxton would place a large order. Chance responded with 1.2-metre sheets.

Paxton also invented machines for shaping sash bars, and he developed a special sash bar that incorporated both an external gutter to carry away rainwater and internal channels to deal with condensation. Components such as these were ideal for mass production to standard sizes. Combined with the cast-iron columns and standard sheets of glass, they formed the basis of a prefabricated building system.

The Crystal Palace Paxton's triumph was a design for the building to house London's 1851 Great Exhibition – the vast, glittering glass structure that became known as the Crystal Palace. Designed at the last minute (Paxton famously did the first sketches on the blotter during a meeting), the Crystal Palace was conceived like one of Paxton's greenhouses. And as a huge aisled building with many standard repeating elements – sashes, gutters, arches, beams, girders, panes of glass – it was an obvious building to be made by prefabrication.

The use of prefabricated components was vital because the exhibition committee had left very little time for the Crystal Palace to be built. Only by manufacturing the parts off-site and transporting them to Hyde Park as they were needed could the great exhibition building be constructed quickly enough. So Paxton arranged a huge logistic exercise. Wrought-iron beams were manufactured by Fox and Henderson in Birmingham; the same firm supplied wooden components from a mill in Chelsea; two factories in Dudley, in the West Midlands, produced the cast-iron columns; glass came from Chance's works, also in Birmingham. Dedicated trains brought the components straight to

...these bright, clean, easily maintained houses were very quickly taken into the hearts of their occupants

Peter Ashley, *More London Peculiars* (on prefabs)

System buildings

The term 'system building' is used today to describe the way in which either entire buildings or large prefabricated components can be factory-made and delivered complete to the site. Buildings or parts are fully finished at the factory and need only to be connected to services to be usable. Many homes, factories, and schools have been built in this way, especially in the 1960s and 1970s, when system building was popular.

the site and they were fixed into place almost as soon as they arrived. The entire job took just nine months.

The Crystal Palace represented the triumph of prefabrication. It showed how buildings could be made from standard components in very little time, and without the disruption caused by the building industry's 'wet' trades. It set the trend for the way railway stations, factories and other utilitarian buildings would be produced in the future.

New initiatives There were manufacturers who shared Paxton's vision poised to seize the opportunities offered by all this publicity. At the same time as Paxton was conceiving his design, Walter Macfarlane, a Glasgow businessman, was preparing his first catalogue of prefabricated buildings – structures made mainly of metal that were sold as flat packs and were shipped far and wide, even to outposts of the British empire. From garden sheds to apartment blocks, from corrugated iron churches to industrial warehouses, prefabrication in its different forms has been widely used ever since.

the condensed idea
Mass production transforms the building process

19 Beaux-arts

The beaux-arts style was a way of building that originated in the school of fine arts set up in Paris in the early 19th century. For the French this carefully composed, highly ornate classical style was closely associated with architectural education. Elsewhere in the world it became an immensely popular style, applied widely to all types of structures, from public buildings to banks.

Like most practitioners of the arts and crafts, architects originally learned their job in a kind of apprenticeship system. A young man (architecture was in its early days an almost exclusively male preserve) would join the office of an established architect and work as a junior, gradually learning the skills of drawing and design. With a good and giving master, it was a system that could work well, but some wanted a more formal system of training leading to a qualification, so that architecture became a profession.

The French academies France was one of the first countries to create such a formal system of teaching architecture. The first French architectural school was the Académie Royale d'Architecture, which was founded in 1671 by Louis XIV's chief financial minister, Jean-Baptiste Colbert.

During the French Revolution, the Académie, with its royal links, was closed, and a few years later, in 1803, Napoleon founded the Ecole des Beaux-Arts to offer training in the fine arts. The school continued to dominate French architectural education throughout the 19th century,

timeline

1803
Napoleon founds the Ecole des Beaux-Arts

1853
The major remodelling of Paris by Baron Haussmann begins, bringing new opportunities for architects to build in the grand style

grand Prix de Rome

The system of awarding the prize of a study-visit to Rome for young architects (and to practitioners of the other arts) was at the heart of French culture. It emphasized that the ultimate foundation of artistic knowledge was to be found in the classical world, and gave the most talented (and those most able to satisfy the tastes of the judges) a direct route to the source. Candidates had first to produce a sketch of their solution to a set design problem. They then worked this up into a more finished presentation called a *charrette* (the world means 'cart', because you needed one to carry your drawings, models and other materials to the presentation), and finally the best eight were selected to work up their ideas into a full project. The winner was sent to Rome for a year to study the architecture and work on their own projects.

but was also increasingly influential in other countries, fostering a style of building that proved popular in the USA, in other American countries and in many parts of Europe.

Spaces and styles The architectural education provided by the Ecole des Beaux-Arts had two influential aspects. First, it promoted a very specific way in which architects were expected to handle space. Students learned to treat the spaces or rooms in a building in a hierarchy, to deploy them symmetrically and to arrange them along axes that passed through the building. They were encouraged to consider the effect these rooms made as one passed from one to another. This way of looking at buildings as series of spaces, and controlling the way these spaces interacted, was hugely influential.

The second aspect of the beaux-arts training was to do with the physical appearance and finish of the buildings. A classical beaux-arts style

1861	1887	1902	1903
Charles Garnier designs the Paris Opera House (now known as the Opéra Garnier)	McKim, Mead and White design the Boston Public Library	McKim, Mead and White design Pennsylvania Station, New York	Charles Mewès and Arthur J. Davis design the Ritz Hotel, London

developed, relying heavily on the influence of classical and neoclassical architecture, and was widely imitated. Buildings were symmetrical, raised on a rusticated lower storey, and eclectically classical. Their style featured roofs hidden behind parapets, rows of often round-headed windows, elaborately treated doorways with classical door cases and the widespread use of classical decorative details, such as pilasters, brackets and cartouches. The beaux-arts architects liked to make their buildings still grander and more ornate with the use of statuary.

Architecture and professionalism

By pioneering architectural education, the beaux-arts school (below) was an important factor in making architecture into a profession. The professional status of architecture in France was confirmed in 1840 when the Société Centrale des Architects was founded. In Britain, the key professional body was the Royal Institute of British Architects (set up in the 19th century), while in America the American Institute of Architects was founded in 1857.

The beaux-arts style flourished in France during the 19th century. It proved ideal for the type of grand public buildings that were put up in increasing numbers in Paris and other major cities – the Opéra Garnier and the Ecole des Beaux-Arts itself are major examples. In England the

> **The Beaux-Arts method was so successful it attracted students from all over the world ...**
>
> John F. Pile, *A History of Interior Design*

style was especially influential in the Edwardian period. As well as one prominent architect, Arthur J. Davis (one of the designers of London's Ritz Hotel), who was educated at the Ecole, many others caught the bug, and elaborate beaux-arts classical buildings became one of the hallmarks of the Edwardian cities.

Beaux-arts outside Europe But the style spread much more widely. It was especially popular in the USA, where architects such as Richard Morris Hunt and the practice of McKim, Mead and White were well known advocates. McKim, Mead and White's enormous Pennsylvania Station in New York (demolished in the 1960s) was one of the greatest examples; Boston Public Library is one of the beaux-arts survivors.

The beaux-arts style spread throughout the world, standing for sophistication and good design wherever Europeans settled and carried their culture – from Argentina to Egypt, Canada to Japan. It survived well into the 20th century because the image it created was popular among all types of clients, from governments to banks. But the style was often bastardized – designers copied the mannerisms and decoration, but ignored the fundamental beaux-arts teaching about the arrangement of spaces. This, and the reliance of the style on lavish decoration, made the beaux-arts manner a target of the modernists, who replaced it with what they saw as a greater awareness of structure and function, and a rejection of ornament. After a long run, beaux-arts had had its day.

the condensed idea
Professional sophistication

20 Arts and Crafts

A number of 19th-century British architects and designers turned away from industry to create a revival of craft-based architecture using local materials. The resulting Arts and Crafts movement was especially strong in England in the last three decades of the 19th century, but its influence was also felt in Europe and, especially, in the USA.

The Victorians were great technologists and restless inventors. Their inventiveness had a huge impact in the construction business, bringing widespread use of materials such as iron in building and developing a range of machines, from steam hoists to improved saws, that made construction faster, easier and more efficient.

But for much of the Victorian period, architects were preoccupied not with technology but with arguments about style. Those who favoured Gothic battled with the classicists; among the 'Goths' debates were rife about which version of Gothic was best; and there were those, rejecting either approach, who preferred the round-arched style of the Normans or the Tudor style that leant itself so well to quaint, timber-framed cottages.

A new start But towards the end of the 19th century a new attitude emerged. Industrial architecture, the argument went, was ugly and inhuman; past styles had more to do with pretension than what people needed in their homes. Instead of these approaches, why not look at the way ordinary country builders worked in the past? They developed their

timeline

1859

Philip Webb designs the Red House, Bexleyheath, Kent, for William Morris and his wife, Jane

1861

The firm of Morris, Marshall, Faulkner & Co is set up, selling hand-made furniture, embroidery, glass, metalwork and other products

craft skills over generations, demonstrating mastery of both tools and materials. Those materials were local, and used with simplicity – houses built this way had plain wooden floors and whitewashed walls inside. But they supplied people's needs perfectly and, at their best, had a beauty that came from the craftsman's skill and the rootedness of the house in its locality.

William Morris The person who led the way in arguing for houses like this was the multitalented designer, artist, writer, teacher and manufacturer William Morris. Morris was not an architect, although he spent a few months working in the office of the great Gothic architect G. E. Street and knew the world of architecture well. And he made it his business, through his work as a manufacturer and designer of all types of items, from fabrics to furniture, to know how craftsmen worked and what they could produce.

Truth to materials

One of the presiding ideas of the Arts and Crafts movement was an interest in, and respect for, materials. From wood to stone, metal to brick, materials were selected with care, preferably from local sources. And finely-forged ironwork (right) or hand-made bricks were not to be covered up – where possible, their beauty should be left exposed so that all could appreciate it. Thus was born the idea that a building should be 'honest', that it should not hide its construction and that it should be, in the phrase popular among both Arts and Crafts and modernist designers, true to its materials.

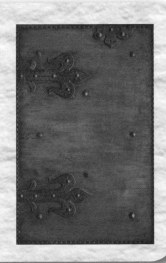

1882	1897	1900	1900–1902
The Century Guild is founded, first of a number of guilds intended to promote craftsmanship	C.F. A. Voysey designs Norney, Shackleford, Surrey	M. H. Baillie Scott designs Blackwell, Bowness on Windermere, Cumbria	W.R. Lethaby designs and builds the church of All Saints, Brockhampton, Herefordshire

Morris spread the word through his writing and lecturing, and by selling the products of his firm – beautifully crafted decorated chests, floral wallpapers and fabrics, some still made today. Other pioneers, including architects such as his friend Philip Webb and the prolific R. Norman Shaw, spread the ideals, especially Shaw, who ran a large office that contained several young men who embraced Arts and Crafts ideals. The Arts and Crafts movement was underway.

Profession or craft? Discussion groups, associations and guilds were formed to discuss the relationship of arts, crafts and architecture. There was something provocative about these discussions because this was a time when many architects were arguing that their work should be a profession – that architects should have the status of doctors or lawyers. It was a case hardly helped by a group of revolutionaries arguing that architecture was not a profession at all, but a craft – like carpentry or ceramics.

However, during the last two decades of the 19th century at least, the revolutionaries demonstrated that they had a point. A succession of stunning houses built using craft techniques, traditional materials and Morrisian principles emerged. Architecture began to look more rooted in locality and site, less cluttered, less formal, than it had for decades. And, although the movement was in many ways a revolt against style, an Arts and Crafts style emerged.

The style was exemplified, in domestic architecture, by the work of architects such as M. H. Baillie Scott and C.F.A. Voysey. Outside: long, low, asymmetrical structures, sweeping roof lines, large bay windows. Inside: exposed wooden floors, pale walls, big inglenook fireplaces, beautiful hand-crafted details, such as specially designed

❛Have nothing in your houses that you do not know to be useful or believe to be beautiful.❜
William Morris

craft guilds

One place where architects and craftsmen came together to discuss each other's work was the craft guilds – specialist societies of which several were founded in the 1880s to promote craftsmanship. The Art Workers' Guild, founded in 1884, was a group including artists, architects and craft workers that met for lectures, discussions, demonstrations of techniques and exhibitions. By contrast, C.R. Ashbee's Guild and School of Handicraft, founded in London in 1888 and moving in 1902 to Chipping Campden in Gloucestershire, was a working body of craftsmen who, in their country home, aimed to revive both the crafts and the skills of husbandry.

door catches or runs of wooden panelling. There was an impeccable logic to all this, too – the asymmetry came from a desire to let the best, most convenient plan dictate the shape of the building; the hand-crafted finish from an overriding respect for the materials themselves.

To begin with this type of design was available mainly to the rich: people who could buy Morris's hand-made objects and who could afford the cost of a one-off house. But the influence lived on and did eventually affect the design of many smaller houses when garden suburbs, such as London's Bedford Park (see pages 196–99), came to be built.

the condensed idea
Craft-based architecture

21 Conservation

During the late 19th century there was a strong reaction against the excessive zeal of church restorers, who often demolished as much of an old building as they repaired. Led by designer, writer and reformer William Morris, this movement led to a new, gentler, less interventionist approach to old buildings. Conservation rather than restoration became the watchword, and people involved in building preservation today still follow the guidelines Morris established.

By the middle of the 19th century a number of people were unhappy with the usual approach taken by architects when restoring old buildings – the approach that involved demolishing parts of a building that were defective or built in some unfashionable style and replacing them with the architect's idea of what was 'correct'. There were several objections to this. It was impossible to tell exactly what was originally there if the surface of a building had worn away, making proper restoration impossible. The approach ironed out the inconsistencies, which were precisely the features of an old building that made it interesting. Much modern masonry had what the critic John Ruskin called a 'brute hardness' when compared to the work of the Middle Ages. And demolition paid scant respect to the craftsmen of the Middle Ages.

William Morris mobilizes These objections came to a head when the great designer, writer and reformer William Morris discovered that Sir George Gilbert Scott was about to begin restoring the great Norman abbey church at Tewkesbury in Gloucestershire.

timeline

1877

William Morris writes a letter to the *Athenaeum*, objecting to the restoration of Tewkesbury Abbey. Soon after, the SPAB is founded

1878

SPAB leaders work out a formal protocol to help them deal with buildings under threat

Having seen what restoration could do to similar buildings, Morris hoped to put a stop to the work. In March 1877 he wrote a letter to the *Athenaeum*:

'My eye just now caught the word "restoration" in the morning paper and, on looking closer, I saw that this time it is nothing less than the minster of Tewkesbury that is to be destroyed by Sir Gilbert Scott. Is it altogether too late to do something to save it – and whatever else is beautiful or historical that is left to us on the sites of the ancient buildings we were once so famous for?'

SPAB precepts

The Society for the Protection of Ancient Buildings is guided by these basic principles:

- Repair not restore.
- Use responsible methods that don't lead to further damage or that cannot be undone in the future.
- Complement not parody: if new work (for example, a new extension) is needed it should be done in a modern architectural idiom, not in an imitation of the old.
- Regular maintenance.

- To understand a building you have to know as much as possible about its use, structure and social importance.
- Do only the work that is absolutely necessary to preserve the building.
- Fit new to old: do not adapt old fabric so that it will accept new fittings.
- Do not try to hide good repairs.
- Respect age: do not 'smooth out' bulges or bows or try to hide the imperfections of age.

1879
Morris and the SPAB take up the campaign to save St Mark's, Venice

1890s
SPAB are advising on nearly 300 buildings per year

1955
The first Threatened Buildings List is published, to find new owners for buildings at risk

> ❝Why, I could carve them better
> with my teeth.❞
>
> **William Morris**
> **(in response to being shown some modern carved stalls in a cathedral)**

A new approach Morris was too late to save Tewkesbury Abbey from Scott's attention – restoration was already under way by the time his letter was published. But Morris was able to set a new standard for the sensitive treatment of old buildings, and he did this by founding the Society for the Protection of Ancient Buildings to guide those caring for the built environment. The SPAB advocated, and still advocates, repair rather than rebuilding, respect for the work of

The shock of the new

When he wrote his manifesto for the SPAB in response to the restoration of Tewkesbury Abbey (right) Morris included one clause that surprised some, encouraging those in charge of an old building 'to raise another building rather than alter or enlarge an old one' if a building became inconvenient for its current use. Morris thus hoped to encourage architects to continue to build anew and, having rejected historical revival for its own sake, would have wanted to see buildings in appropriate current styles.

ancient artists and artisans, resistance to tampering with old fabric to make it consistent, and 'honesty' – one should not try to disguise new work as old.

In putting forward these new ideas, Morris and his followers had to counter two persistent trends in contemporary thinking. First, when it came to church restoration, it had been thought acceptable to demolish part of an old building if it was deemed to be inappropriate for modern ritual. Morris held that ancient buildings were sacred, and should not be altered to suit passing liturgical fashion. Second, historical revival, so popular among Victorian architects, was not necessarily a good thing if it meant damaging ancient fabric.

Friends and supporters Such revolutionary ideas would have had little chance of support had they come from Morris alone. But fortunately Morris had the backing of several architects, including his friend Philip Webb and the visionary Arts and Crafts architect, teacher and writer W.R. Lethaby. With this backing the SPAB was born and began to attract members from within the architectural profession.

Slowly, approaches to the upkeep of old buildings changed from restoration to conservation. And broadly speaking this is the approach that still prevails today. SPAB undertakes training, gives advice on conservation, publishes books, campaigns on behalf of old buildings and takes part in the planning system to ensure that old buildings are properly preserved. Its principles and practices are now followed widely. We end up with better, and better maintained, buildings as a result.

the condensed idea
TLC for old buildings

22 The City Beautiful

There is something very distinctive about the grid plans of American cities, but also something limited. At the end of the 19th century a group of American planners tried to open up the grid plan, providing baroque elements such as grand plazas and diagonal boulevards to produce what they called the City Beautiful.

In the 1870s and 80s one of the most successful North American architects was Henry Hobson Richardson. Although he trained at the Ecole des Beaux-Arts in Paris, Richardson's favourite style was not beaux-arts classicism but a form of round-arched massive style that owed a lot to the Romanesque buildings of 10th- and 11th-century Europe. He designed fine churches and public buildings such as libraries in this style, and his type of architecture, which historians have called both massive and masculine, became popular in the USA, especially in Chicago and the Midwest.

A force for change But in 1893 a reaction began. This was the year in which the World's Columbian Exposition was held in Chicago. This was a prestige event, held to attract foreign business to the USA in the wake of an economic depression, and both local Chicago architects and firms from the Eastern cities were invited to design the buildings.

timeline

1893	1901–2	1903
World's Columbian Exposition held in Chicago	Burnham, McKim, and F L Olmsted Jr draw up a new plan for Washington D.C. inspired by L'Enfant's original scheme for the city	Charles Mulford Robinson publishes *Modern Civic Art, or the City Made Beautiful*

World's Fairs

The World's Columbian Exposition in Chicago (right) was one of a number of large-scale international trade fairs held throughout the 19th and early 20th centuries. Among the most famous were, as well as the Chicago fair, the London Great Exhibition of 1851, another London exhibition in 1861, the Philadelphia Exhibition of 1876, the Melbourne Exhibition of 1880 and a string of exhibitions in Paris from 1855 to 1900. These were showpieces of manufacturing, promoting international trade. They could also be showcases of architecture, bringing innovative or traditional design to the attention of thousands of visitors. Both the London 1851 exhibition, with its Crystal Palace (see page 74), and the Paris Universal Exhibition of 1889 had famous metal and glass buildings. Others, such as Chicago's, promoted a grander, more traditional style of architecture.

The overall plan of the Exposition site, laid out by the great landscape architect and reformer Frederick Law Olmsted and the architect Burnham along beaux-arts lines, centred on a 'Court of Honor' around a lake. Many of the buildings on the site were classical, lined with

1903–6

Cass Gilbert works on a plan for the surroundings of the Minnesota State Capitol, St Paul

1904–5

Burnham and Edward H. Bennett create a new plan for San Francisco

1906–9

Burnham and Bennett create a new plan for Chicago

> **❝The civic centre's beauty would reflect the souls of the city's inhabitants, inducing order, calm, and propriety therein.❞**
>
> **William H. Wilson,**
> **The City Beautiful Movement**

columns, and topped with domes. Their stone was mostly white and their elegant, pale, classical appearance soon earned the Exposition site the nickname 'The White City'. It was hugely influential, turning many American architects away from Richardson's ponderous Chicago style to something more classical, and more influenced by the Parisian beaux-arts.

A new approach to planning It was not just the style of the buildings, but the whole attitude to city planning that was affected, in a trend that became known as the City Beautiful movement. Architects and planners had realized that, although American cities generally had grid plans, which in theory could be extended ad infinitum, most had no proper plans for expansion, often no proper city planning at all. The City Beautiful was an answer to this lack.

The planners of the City Beautiful movement proposed to break through the grid plans of American cities with bold diagonal avenues and boulevards, to create dramatic vistas in the grand manner, and to include parks and trees to make the city greener. Planners found an American blueprint for this type of city in the original plan, made by Frenchman Pierre Charles L'Enfant, for Washington D.C. in the late 18th century. This plan, with its tree-lined streets and rond-points, was followed only loosely, but the City Beautiful planners revived it, aiming to add a touch of the baroque to the grid-based regularity of American cities.

Grand plans Architect Daniel Burnham was the greatest advocate of the City Beautiful. His 1909 plan for Chicago sees the city sliced through with a series of new diagonal streets converging on a piazza containing the new City Hall. Burnham praised such diagonals as segregating traffic and taking it to the centre as rapidly as possible. He also claimed that the triangular blocks created by diagonals were a golden opportunity to design unusually shaped public buildings.

A few American cities, such as Milwaukee and Madison, Wisconsin, were given their share of diagonal streets and grand-manner planning. Some gained boulevards, graceful tree-lined streets, with tree-planted median strips, often connecting parks and leading out to the suburbs. In these outer areas such streets became 'parkways', genteel streets with views over the landscape. This kind of green planning, already made popular by Frederick Law Olmsted, was also fostered by Burnham and other followers of the City Beautiful movement.

Civic centres The City Beautiful planners also used diagonal streets to emphasize city centres. Public buildings should be collected together around a central piazza, to which the diagonals unerringly led. There would be public statues and fountains, and the city halls, libraries, museums and other buildings would be arranged around the square in a harmonious way – not just plonked down according to convenience on the grid, as often happened in American cities.

From Elgin, Illinois, to Cedar Rapids, Iowa, many of the plans of the City Beautiful advocates went unrealized. Without supreme power it proved impossible to sweep away city blocks for the sake of vistas in the grand manner. But the idea of a civic centre, combining governmental and cultural buildings – something that was achieved in major cities such as San Francisco – had a lasting legacy on American planning, adding beauty and elegance to urban centres, and saying something powerful about what an American city should be like.

the condensed idea
Grand-manner city planning

23 Art Nouveau

One of the strongest reactions against the clutter, formality and artistic revivalism of the Victorian period was Art Nouveau – a style of art that swept across Europe between about 1890 and 1905. Its natural motifs and sinuous curves transformed architecture in cites from Prague to Paris, and the movement proved a rich begetter of local variations, including the more rectilinear styles that caught on in Austria.

Several different influences caused artists to create the Art Nouveau style. One came from the ideas of William Morris and John Ruskin, who reacted against Victorian art with a call for less clutter and more investigation of natural forms. Another was a new fashion in Europe for Japanese art, with its strong graphic content and rich colours. A third was the work of the Czech artist Alfons Mucha, whose posters, much used in major international centres such as Paris, stimulated a fashion for sinuous curves, images of flowers and portrayals of sensuous feminine beauty.

Graphic roots Graphics were an area in which Art Nouveau motifs could be worked out and developed, and another strong influence was a book cover for a volume called *Wren's City Churches*, designed by architect A.H. Mackmurdo. Dating from 1883, this design features flowers and strong curving stems and leaves in bold monochrome. Because it appeared on the front of a book about architecture that many

timeline

1883	1893
Wren's City Churches published in Britain	Tassel House, Brussels, designed by Victor Horta

The Vienna Secession

A crisis occurred in the arts in Vienna in around 1898 when a group of artists broke away, or seceded, from the establishment to form the movement called the Secession. The group's most prominent architect was Joseph Maria Olbrich who, partly influenced by Scotsman Charles Rennie Mackintosh, developed a strong rectilinear style adorned with contrasting flowing Art Nouveau ornament. Olbrich's most famous work is the Secession Building in Vienna, where the group held exhibitions. It has a dome covered with laurel leaf decoration.

British architects must have bought, it was a strong influence on the curves and forms of architectural Art Nouveau.

Architects picked up on these influences in different ways. Frenchman Hector Guimard explored the use of colourful materials, such as faience, and transformed Paris with the dramatic curving ironwork of his Métro station entrances. Belgian Henry van de Velde began as an artist and book designer before bringing the long curves of Art Nouveau to wall decoration and structural details, such as the shapes of roofs. Another Belgian, Victor Horta, followed in his footsteps. The style also spread to Germany, where it was known as the Jugendstil. Further east, cities such as Prague, Moscow and Riga became centres of Art Nouveau decoration.

In England the movement had a greater influence on product design than on architecture. One area in which it was influential was pottery, and firms such as Doulton, who made vases and other pottery for the

1897	1898	1899–1904	1907
Charles Rennie Mackintosh begins work on the Glasgow School of Art buildings	Vienna Secession formed	Hector Guimard designs station entrances for the Paris Métro	Gaudí's Casa Mila, Barcelona, completed

Art Nouveau and the crafts

Although most Art Nouveau buildings had conventional structures, the movement took advantage of both craft and industrial technology for their ornamental work. Decorative tiles were common on British Art Nouveau buildings, while French Art Nouveau structures, such as the Paris Métro station entrances (below) used ironwork creatively, with ornate panels, curving rails and metal-framed canopies. The art of lettering and typography also formed an important element in the station entrances.

home as well as ceramic tiles for buildings, made a big impact. Their tiles proved popular for exterior cladding on buildings from factories to shops, and some of their designs bore Art Nouveau motifs, such as foliage, hearts and whiplash curves.

Scotland had a major Art Nouveau architect in Charles Rennie Mackintosh. The most famous of his stunning buildings is Glasgow School of Art. His style is based on straight lines and meticulous patterning. Mackintosh's rectilinear form of Art Nouveau bears a strong resemblance to the Austrian version of the style. Known as Secessionist, the design and architecture of Austrian *fin de siècle* is highly distinctive.

A city style The influence of Art Nouveau was strongest in the cities, where it was used most widely for the design of upper-class houses and for buildings such as hotels, where good, up-to-date decor was at a premium to attract rich and sophisticated clients. Its curves were more useful in decoration than in laying out buildings, most of which have walls and partitions made up of straight lines and right-angles. But one architect, heavily influenced by Art Nouveau, took the idea of the use of curves further than any other. Antoni Gaudí, the great Catalan architect who worked in Barcelona, was a complete individual. His buildings, with their curving walls, pillars like stalagmites, colourful tile mosaics and irregular windows, are like the work of no other architect.

> **'... the terrifying and edible beauty of Art Nouveau architecture.'**
> **Salvador Dalí**

Gaudí's eccentric and irregular forms, with their sweeping curves, are very much influenced by Art Nouveau and its Catalan incarnation, which was known as Modernisme. Gaudí's extraordinary apartment blocks, his bizarre and colourful garden buildings and his great church of the Sagrada Familia make up one of the most impressive bodies of work of any architect. They would have been impossible without roots in Art Nouveau.

A passing vogue Art Nouveau was a short-lived movement. Its heyday was past by 1905, although some designs continued to show an Art Nouveau influence in the following years. But it was more important than its short vogue suggests, because it was a way of making a decisive break from the past forms and the artistic revivals that had dominated the previous decades. It restored the notion of the shock of the new to architecture, and prepared architects and clients alike for the yet more shocking architecture of the 20th century.

the condensed idea
Flowing curves, natural beauty

24 Garden city

In the 1870s a number of landlords and social reformers began to design improved housing for ordinary people, creating spacious settlements with generous gardens that became the first 'garden suburbs'. At the end of the century this idea was developed and extended into the garden city movement, with the creation of entire new towns that had a lasting influence on the way housing developments were planned.

The movement began with the garden suburb, an idea that has its roots in the Arts and Crafts movement and in the 'Domestic Revival' architecture – a mixture of Tudor, vernacular and Queen Anne – of the 1870s and 1880s. An early example was the West London suburb of Bedford Park. Begun in 1875 Bedford Park was a series of tree-lined streets meeting at a village centre containing the station, shops, inn and church. There was plenty of greenery and the houses had large gardens. The houses themselves – many of which were designed by Norman Shaw – combined red brick, timber and inventive elevations with bay windows, porches and other interesting details – in other words they were the essence of the style that came to be known as Queen Anne.

Other communities along similar lines appeared, most notably Bournville, the industrial garden village built by the Cadbury chocolate company for their employees. While Bedford Park, with its mainly large houses, was emphatically middle class, Bournville cast its social net more widely, with accommodation for workers on different levels of the Cadbury's hierarchy. The place grew, too, with more houses and

timeline

1875
Planning of the London suburb of Bedford Park is begun

1879
Cadbury's move their factory to Bournville, near Birmingham, and the first houses there are built

The social mix

Pioneers such as Ebenezer Howard saw themselves as social reformers. They wanted to improve people's lives and create better societies by planning suburbs and cities in innovative ways. They encouraged such beneficial activities as getting out in the fresh air and growing vegetables in the garden. They also tried to promote a good social mix, providing houses of different sizes, so that rich and poor could live close by, as they tend to do in a city centre.

buildings, such as schools and churches, being built in the decades after its foundation in 1879.

The vision of Ebenezer Howard Settlements such as Bedford Park and Bournville influenced the pioneer planner Ebenezer Howard, but his vision was larger. He wanted entire cities to be built on these principles, with generous planting, plenty of space and community facilities. He wanted something else, too: a type of planning logic that reflected his values of community. Howard was convinced that garden cities were the cities for tomorrow.

In 1898 Howard published his ideas in a book called *Tomorrow; a Peaceful Path to Real Reform*. The book was reprinted four years later under the title *Garden Cities of Tomorrow*. Howard was convinced that both town and country had their attractions and wanted to bring both together in a new type of city. It would be as pleasant to live in as a garden settlement, such as Bedford Park or Bournville, but because it was a city it needed to be larger and contain community facilities, such as museums and libraries, a hospital and a town hall. And because

1898	**1903**	**1907**	**1919**
First edition of Ebenezer Howard's *Tomorrow; a Peaceful Path to Real Reform* is published	Work begins on the new town of Letchworth	Work on the new town of Hellerau, Germany, is begun	Work begins on Welwyn Garden City

The English House

The skill of British builders in creating well-designed housing for all social classes impressed the government in Prussia so much that they sent the architect Hermann Muthesius on a fact-finding tour to the country in the 1890s. Muthesius studied all types of houses, large and small, but was especially impressed with the architecture of Bedford Park (right) and Bournville. He included examples of both in his long, three-volume study, *Das englische Haus* (The English House), which appeared in 1904–5 and immediately became a standard work on English domestic architecture. The book helped spread the ideas and aesthetics of British housing into mainland Europe.

Howard could see clearly the advantages of keeping city and country in close proximity, the garden city contained not only parks and gardens, but also, on its edges, allotments and dairy farms, with larger farms just beyond its edges.

The concentric plan Howard laid these diverse elements out in a circular town plan that was both beautiful and logical. At the very centre was a garden, from which a number of boulevards radiated, like the spokes of a wheel. In a circle around the garden were the major public buildings – town hall, concert hall, theatre, library, hospital, museum – and in a broad ring around them was a large, central park. Concentric rings of avenues containing houses and schools followed, and beyond them were a railway line, allotments and dairy farms.

Greening the city Howard's design was revolutionary. Most city dwellers at the end of the 19th century had to put up with cramped conditions and treeless streets. Howard's proposed city would give them a sense of space, greenery and state-of-the-art public facilities. But in the Britain of the late 19th century the emphasis was on adding to existing towns rather than building entirely new cities, so there seemed little prospect that Howard's vision of tomorrow would ever be built. Garden cities were built in Germany, though. Hellerau, which was begun in 1907 near Dresden, and Neudorf, Strasbourg, begun in 1912, were notable examples.

> **'Town and country must be married, and out of this joyous union will spring new hope, a new life, a new civilization.'**
>
> Ebenezer Howard,
> *Garden Cities of Tomorrow*

In Britain, two new towns drew on Howard's ideas: Letchworth, begun in 1903, and Welwyn Garden City, laid out in the early 1920s. Letchworth – with its curving streets, neo-Tudor houses and greenery – is close to Howard's ideals and to the principles of developments such as Bedford Park. Welwyn is planned along similar lines, but by the time it was built the neo-Tudor style had been replaced by a type of imitation Georgian.

The ideals of Howard and his ideas lived on – not in further new towns, but in countless estates and suburbs built on to existing cities. Curving streets and closes, green spaces and neo-Tudor or neo-Georgian houses proved a winning formula for the large amounts of social housing that were needed after the Second World War. Developments such as these from the 1920s and 30s still prove popular with tenants and planners alike.

the condensed idea
Nature comes to town

25 Skyscraper

Although the cathedral builders of the Middle Ages had known how to build tall towers and spires, the search for ways to build practical tall buildings to house offices and apartments began in the late 19th century. The result was the skyscraper, developed in America before becoming one of the world's most distinctive urban building types.

In the 1850s and 60s, with the arrival of the railroad and the development of lumbering and meat-processing plants, Chicago became one of the most important cities of the USA. But in 1871 disaster struck in the form of a fire that swept through a large part of the city centre. Rebuilding was soon underway.

Fireproof construction The first priority was to construct fireproof buildings using materials such as stone and brick instead of wood. Fireproof construction was more costly than people were used to paying for domestic buildings, so this pushed up prices in the downtown fire-damaged area and turned it into a district almost exclusively filled with commercial and administrative buildings. The cost, plus the demand for land in this business district, imposed on developers a second imperative: to pack as much accommodation as possible into this valuable city land. The way to do this was to build tall.

So it was that in the decades after the fire the world's first skyscrapers – tall buildings based on a framework of steel – were built in Chicago. They transformed the city and gave the world an entirely new type of architecture, one that would dominate big-city building for much of

timeline

1854	1871
Elisha Graves Otis demonstrates his safety elevator at the New York Crystal Palace Exhibition	A major city fire stimulates redevelopment in Chicago

the 20th century. The first of them, the modest ten-storey Home Insurance Company building of 1885, was designed by William Le Baron Jenney, a Chicago architect who was also an engineer, and so ideally qualified for the job. So by modern standards the early Chicago skyscrapers were not particularly tall, but they pointed the way towards future taller buildings constructed on similar principles.

The safety elevator

The pulley is an ancient invention, and combined with a power source – from a steam engine to an electric motor – it could be used to power a hoist to lift loads from one floor of a building to another. But if the rope broke, the goods fell to the bottom, making the hoist unsafe for human passengers. The problem was solved by Elisha Graves Otis (right), who devised a safety elevator, on which pawls (hinged catches) on the elevator cage were forced by springs to engage ratchets if the rope broke. The ratchets caught the cage and passengers were saved from a fatal plunge. Otis convinced sceptics by riding his device himself and ordering the rope to be severed.

1885
The Chicago Home Insurance Company Building is the first skeleton-framed skyscraper

1894–5
The Reliance Building, Chicago, constructed

1913
The 55-storey Woolworth Building is the first of New York's great skyscrapers

1931
Empire State Building becomes the world's tallest skyscraper

> **❛The [steel] frame has become the catalyst of an architecture.❜**
>
> Colin Rowe, *The Architectural Review*, 1956

A meeting of technologies What was distinctively different about the early skyscrapers was something more subtle than mere height. It was the coming together of several different technologies to make a tall building possible – plumbing and heating systems that could cope with a big building, the steel frame and the safety elevator. With all these things in place, together with the power hoists and other equipment that was developing in the construction industry at this time, the skyscraper could begin its steady rise to prominence.

Skyscraper architecture As skyscrapers grew, the patterns of skyscraper architecture began to emerge. Because they were always major engineering projects, tall buildings were often designed by men like Jenney, who combined the skills of architect and engineer, or by firms such as Holabird and Roche or Burnham and Root (both of Chicago), who could provide practitioners of both disciplines. Such firms often produced tall buildings that had little ornament – their effects came from mass rather than decoration.

When heights increased, skyscrapers often tapered towards the top, reaching a point by way of a series of setbacks that both enhanced their form and helped admit natural light to the streets below. Setbacks like this were eventually incorporated into planning laws in cities such as New York.

Floor plans Another common thread in the design of these buildings was in the floor plans. The constant element was the shaft containing the elevators, which was often in the middle of the floor area (or sometimes at one end). The rest of the floor area could be divided by partition walls or left undivided – walls were not vital structurally because the steel framework supported the weight of the

The curtain wall

In a skyscraper the weight of the building is taken on a framework of steel. The walls do not have to bear a large load – their main purpose is to insulate the building. Early skyscrapers had walls of various materials from bricks to glazed terracotta panels. Later skyscrapers often had a skin made up almost entirely of panels of glass – a type of surface known as a curtain wall – suspended from the outer part of the framework. This type of design was admired both for its light-filled interiors and its gleaming exterior.

building. An advantage of placing the elevator shafts in the middle of the building was that it freed up the 'outer' parts of each floor, where natural light was more plentiful, for office accommodation.

The race to be tallest As engineers perfected the design of steel frames, building grew taller and height became a goal in itself. A race to build the world's tallest skyscraper was won by New York's Empire State Building, which reached a height of 318 metres (1,044 ft) – a title it held for more than 40 years.

By this time skyscrapers had become far more than a way of using technology to cram a lot of offices into a tight space. They were symbols of engineering achievement and commercial success. And so they continue, as growing economies from Dubai to Shanghai once more compete to build tall.

the condensed idea
Using steel to build tall

26 Futurism

Italian futurism began as a movement of artists and writers and spread to architecture in the visionary work of Antonio Sant'Elia. Although he built little and lost his life in the First World War, Sant'Elia produced stunning architectural drawings that had a lasting influence on later architects, including members of the modernist movement and practitioners of Art Deco.

The phrase 'movers and shakers' is rather overused, but it does contain an important notion: that every so often a person or a group of people comes along who change history by shaking things up and moving things along. They do not necessarily produce very much, but they make a lot of noise and make people think. Nowhere is this more true than in the case of the artistic movement known as futurism.

The futurist manifesto Futurism began in 1909 as a movement of writers and artists. Like many people at around this time, the first futurists, who came from Italy, believed that the current art was outmoded and unfit for purpose in the modern world of the still young 20th century. Writer Filippo Tommaso Marinetti launched their movement with a manifesto, published in an Italian newspaper on 5 February 1909 and then in France, in *Le Figaro*, two weeks later.

In the manifesto Marinetti and his followers renounced the past. They wanted art that was young and daring and original – even if that originality involved violence. They celebrated technology and speed –

timeline

1909
Original futurist manifesto published in *La Gazzetta dell'Emilia*

1912
Antonio Sant'Elia begins to make futurist drawings of city buildings

they loved cars and aeroplanes – and were so besotted with everything fast, sudden and violent that they even promised to glorify war in their art.

An architecture for the future These ideas, absurd and overblown in themselves, produced some striking paintings of running figures, speeding cyclists and pulsating cities. They also inspired an Italian architect, Antonio Sant'Elia, to invent a futurist architecture. Like Marinetti, Sant'Elia produced a manifesto (the futurists favoured such documents) to explain his ideas. It calls for an architecture for the future, one that renounces the historical styles and ornament that were current in Europe in favour of an unornamented, bold new way of building. Futurist architecture, says the manifesto, should draw its effects from the frank use of modern materials (concrete, glass, steel) and the daring use of striking forms.

Sant'Elia went on to explain the aesthetics that the proper use of these materials would generate. The futurist city would be 'like an immense and tumultuous shipyard, active, mobile, and everywhere dynamic, and the modern building like a gigantic machine'. Technology, instead of being hidden away, should be displayed and celebrated – so elevators, for example, should 'swarm up façades like serpents of glass and iron'. Conveyor belts (high-speed, of course) and catwalks would deal with traffic.

"A racing car . . . is more beautiful than the Victory of Samothrace."

Filippo Tommaso Marinetti, *Futurist Manifesto*

1914	1914	1916	1933
Sant'Elia's drawings of La Città Nuova are shown in an exhibition called Nuove Tendenze in Milan	The futurist architectural manifesto is compiled by Sant'Elia, probably with the help of Marinetti	Sant'Elia is killed during fighting on the Trieste front during the First World War	Santa Maria Novella station, Florence, is completed

Architecture should take over not just the ground and the space above it, said Sant'Elia, but should also burrow into it: buildings should 'plunge storey deep into the earth'. And ornament should be replaced by a scientific approach to building, in which beauty would emerge through the logical lines and masses of the buildings. Architects should abandon their love of decoration, mouldings, porticoes and other antique details, and place their faith in the grouping of masses on a grand scale.

Drawing the future The past, then, was laid aside, and the aim was to find a new way of building that truly lived up to modern needs, modern technology and the pace of modern life. Sant'Elia developed these ideas in a breathtaking series of drawings of cities – the drawings may have come before the manifesto, but this is not known for sure.

Sant'Elia's drawings depict not just skyscrapers, but also building types of the 20th century – airports, power stations and so on. Most dramatic are grand apartment buildings, with tall, stepped façades, sweeping roadways and narrow bridges, and dramatic, towering railway stations.

The futurists liked to portray their movement as coming from their own thoughts alone, and representing a complete turning-away from past and present architecture. But Sant'Elia's drawings owe something to the skylines of American cities, especially New York. They are unique, though, and have been widely admired since they were shown in an exhibition called Nuove Tendenze in 1914.

A changed world But they are only drawings. Sant'Elia joined the Italian army and was killed in the First World War before he had the chance to build much. When the war ended in 1918, the world seemed a different place, and in architecture the time for the outrageous claims of the futurists seemed long gone. But architects remembered Sant'Elia's drawings, and his ideas about the coming together of technology and an ornament-free machine aesthetic. His ideas had an influence on the more straight-laced designs of the

The lingering influence

A number of Italian buildings of the period after the First World War show the influence of the ideas of Marinetti and Sant'Elia. In keeping with the futurists' glorification of speed and transport, among the most notable are railway stations, especially the ones at Trento and Florence (Santa Maria Novella). At Santa Maria Novella (below), designed by Giovanni Michelucci, and built in 1932–3, great sweeps of glazing and strong, simple masses certainly recall the futurists. So, too, does the fact that special access roads and parking areas ensure that the car is as well accommodated in this station as the trains.

modernist architects of the 1920s and 1930s. His sense of drama probably also influenced those who wanted to find a modern route to grand effects – from the architects of Art Deco to Ridley Scott in the film 'Blade Runner'. Even in the 1980s the future seemed futurist.

the condensed idea
Bulldoze the past

27 Expressionism

The expressionist movement had its heyday in Germany and the Netherlands in the 1920s. It brought dramatic new forms – curving walls and faceted domes, for example – to modern architecture, giving architects and clients new ideas about how concrete, in particular, might be used. Its ideas lived on to influence some of the more dramatic buildings of the 1950s and 1960s.

The most famous architecture of the period between the two World Wars is in the modernist mode, building that uses materials such as steel, glass and concrete to create mainly rectilinear forms. The architecture of the Bauhaus (see pages 120–123) and of the so-called 'International Style' (see page 124–127) falls into this category. But there was a different tendency, in which materials such as concrete were used to create more organic, sculptural, and sometimes symbolic, forms. This type of architecture has been called 'expressionism'.

New shapes and forms Whereas the buildings of the Bauhaus and International Style were all straight lines and seemed to result from a rational approach to construction, expressionist architecture embraced curves and flowing forms that seemed to bend like rubber, or crystalline forms that reflected the light in a myriad surfaces of glass. It was a type of architecture that gloried in the new shapes and forms that were possible with modern materials.

The main exponents of this type of building were Dutch and German architects and its first major project was a theatre, the Grosse

timeline

1914

The Glass Pavilion, Cologne, erected to the design of Bruno Taut

1918

In Amsterdam architect Piet Kramer designs an expressionist housing scheme in brick

Schauspielhaus, built in Berlin after the First World War and designed by Hans Poelzig. The auditorium of this building was dominated by an extraordinary plaster ceiling with rows and rows of pendants that hung down like stalactites. The effect was further heightened by thousands of coloured light bulbs.

czech cubism

One precursor of expressionism is the Czech architectural style known as cubism. In the early 20th century, many Czech artists travelled in Europe, seeking inspiration in centres such as Paris and Munich. When cubist painting began to be exhibited in Paris in 1908, it inspired not only painters from Prague, but also Czech architects. They saw that the broken or prismatic picture planes of Picasso and Braque could be adapted to create similarly prismatic building façades. Architects such as Jan Kotera and Pavel Janák designed buildings full of acute angles and sometimes irregular forms, which formed radical departures from both the classicism and the highly ornate Art Nouveau then fashionable in Prague.

1919
The Grosse Schauspielhaus, Berlin, Germany, designed by Hans Poelzig, is completed

1921
Erich Mendelsohn's Einstein Tower, Potsdam, Germany, is completed

1928
Rudolf Steiner's Goetheanum, Dornach, is built

> **A man of genius must constantly renew himself, otherwise he is ossified.**
>
> Erich Mendelsohn

Other types of building Curves and glittering lights seemed appropriate for the interior of a theatre, a type of space in which lavish decoration and fantasy had always been acceptable. But the expressionists also produced designs for more mundane buildings – Hans Bernhard Sharoun's project for a stock exchange and Erich Mendelsohn's drawings of factories, film studios and other buildings are notable examples. All demonstrate the possibilities for curving, organic forms offered by steel and concrete.

Erich Mendelsohn's most famous building, the Einstein Tower at Potsdam, Germany, is just such a study in curved form. This structure consists of a tower containing an observatory above a low structure containing a laboratory and sleeping accommodation for the people who worked there. The entire structure is a study in curves, and looks as if it has been made by pouring concrete into vast rubber moulds. In fact its underlying structure is actually of brick, with the concrete added as a smooth finish.

Crystalline buildings There was a contrary tendency in expressionism, in which instead of curves, small crystalline facets made up the surface of the building. An early example was the Glass Pavilion in Cologne, designed by Bruno Taut and built in 1914. This was a round, compact building that formed part of an exhibition site, and its most stunning feature was its domed roof, shaped rather like half a lemon and made up of dozens of large diamond-shaped glass panes.

Panes of glass could shine like the facets of a jewel, but walls could be treated in a faceted way, too, folding in and out at odd angles as if they were made of cardboard rather than concrete. The buildings of the Czech cubist movement look rather like this, as does the Goetheanum at Dornach designed by a man who was not an architect at all, the philosopher, writer and teacher Rudolf Steiner. This so-called 'spiritual high school' is all angles and concrete ribs rising to a bizarre domed roof. There is no doubt that Steiner saw the expressionist mode as giving him

gaudí

The celebrated Catalan architect Antoni Gaudí combined a mixture of influences – from Gothic to Art Nouveau – to forge a unique style that can be seen as a form of expressionism. Gaudí's daring structures, in which walls curve and bulge, columns tilt or splay outwards, and features such as towers and windows take on weird, organic forms certainly mirror the sculptural quality of expressionism. However, many of his most celebrated projects in this mode, such as his two Barcelona blocks of luxury apartments, the Casa Milá and Casa Batlló, were both completed under the influence of Art Nouveau before the First World War and the rise of expressionism in northern Europe.

the chance to express the distinctive nature of his ideas in physical form, an alternative architecture for an alternative philosophy.

The idea lives on Expressionist architecture was not a coherent style with schools and manifestos like the Bauhaus. It was more a tendency pursued by a number of innovative architects who wanted to explore the possibilities of modern materials. Unlike the International Style, it did not produce thousands of followers in the mid-century, but it did have an enduring influence. The sculptural forms of Art Deco owe something to expressionism.

And a number of buildings put up in the decades after the Second World War explored the expressive possibilities of concrete and other materials in ways that the expressionist architects would have recognized. Le Corbusier's small, sculptural pilgrimage chapel at Ronchamp, France, and Sydney's famous Opera House designed by Jørn Utzon, are both examples of buildings that extend the ideas of expressionism long after the heyday of the movement in Germany.

the condensed idea
Architecture as sculpture

28 De Stijl

Dutch architects were in the vanguard of modernism from 1910 to the end of the 1920s. Their De Stijl movement, which produced stunning white houses of great refinement, had a strong influence on the Bauhaus and other schools of design, and architects still learn much, both from its careful handling of space and its attention to details and furnishing.

While much of Europe was in the turmoil of the First World War, the Netherlands was a neutral power and the country's artists and architects took the opportunity to pursue a kind of modernism that was in some ways more refined and advanced than any other. They reduced painting to an arrangement of straight lines and colours and distilled architecture into its constituent parts – planes and spaces. The movement they formed had the simplest of names, reflecting the apparent simplicity of their work: it was called De Stijl, the Style.

The work of Mondrian It began with painting, especially with the work of Piet Mondrian. Having begun, under the influence of the cubists, to break down his paintings into arrangements – still representational – of straight lines, Mondrian simplified his work still further. The typical Mondrian canvas consisted of black vertical and horizontal lines, the rectangles between them filled with white or with primary colours. These arrangements had a spiritual significance for Mondrian. As well as breaking painting down to its basic parts, he was also pursuing a higher truth – a type of spiritual geometry.

The influence of Frank Lloyd Wright Mondrian, a painter, worked in two dimensions. But the artists of De Stijl found three-

timeline

1916

Robert van't Hoff builds concrete houses near Utrecht that are influenced by van Doesburg's ideas and prefigure the De Stijl movement

1917

De Stijl movement founded by Theo van Doesburg

dimensional inspiration in another source: the buildings of Frank Lloyd Wright in America.

The modern Dutch architects seized on Wright's flair with interlocking planes and fluid interior spaces. They appreciated the big verandas and overhanging roofs of buildings such as Wright's Robie House in Chicago. And they liked the way Wright designed every detail of his houses. They ignored what was more old-fashioned about Wright – the Arts and Crafts influence and the use of ornament.

Space and spirit The architect members of the group were Theo van Doesburg, J.J.P. Oud, Gerrit Rietveld, Cornelis van Eesteren and Robert van't Hoff. They took the pared-down approach of Mondrian, adding the spatial flexibility of Wright. They looked for purity and simplicity of form, but also for spiritual meaning. So a typical De Stijl house is built up of a series of interlocking planes – sections of wall,

Spiritual or pragmatic?

From almost the beginning there was a split in the ideas of the De Stijl movement. On the one hand, van Doesburg, the movement's great theorist, insisted that architecture should have spiritual meaning. He used elements such as colour to build this extra dimension, and saw architecture as a high calling that should take buildings beyond the immediate physical needs of clients. J.J.P. Oud, on the other hand, stressed the importance of the social needs of the people who used his buildings. He left the movement in the early 1920s to pursue his more pragmatic vision, although his houses were still influenced by the powerful composition of De Stijl architecture.

1917–18	**1921**	**1924**	**1931**
Gerrit Rietveld designs his Red-Blue Chair	Van Doesburg lectures at the Bauhaus, spreading De Stijl ideas	Gerrit Rietveld's Schröder House, Utrecht, is completed	Van Doesburg dies and the group is disbanded

> **6 . . . a style now ripening, based on a pure equivalence between the age and its means of expression . . .9**
>
> **Theo van Doesburg,** printed in the periodical *De Stijl*

floor, overhanging roof and so on, mostly coloured white but with the occasional dash of pure, primary colour. Many of these planes seem to float in space, giving the building an insubstantial quality.

Inside, there is a free flow of space, sometimes with movable partitions rather than permanent walls between rooms. Large windows help interior and garden spaces meet and blend. Structures such as glass stairs also open up the interior space, as well as giving it a sense of magic. At the same time the strong horizontals and verticals – including glazing bars, balcony rails, and radiator pipes – provide a sense of containment, like the black lines in a Mondrian painting.

Architects' furniture

Many architects – for example, followers of the Arts and Crafts movement, modernists such as Mies van der Rohe, and members of De Stijl – saw a building as a total work of art. They argued that the architect should design everything in a building, and this included not just fittings but also furniture. As a result many modern architects made striking furniture designs for use in their buildings, and these items also became popular more widely. Mies's metal-and-leather Barcelona Chair, originally made for the German Pavilion at the Barcelona Exposition and then widely copied, is the most famous example. Gerrit Rietveld's Red-Blue Chair (right), a structure of planes and lines like a three-dimensional Mondrian painting, symbolizes De Stijl for many people.

> **Masses shoot in all directions – forwards, backwards, to the right, to the left … In this way, modern architecture will increasingly develop into a process of reduction to positive proportion …**

J. J. P. Oud

This highly refined type of design reached its most achieved form in the Schröder House, Utrecht, built by Gerrit Rietveld for Mme Schröder, an artist, in 1923–4. The building is small, but beautifully finished, and the attention to detail is such that most of the fixtures and fittings were designed by the architect himself. The house was furnished with De Stijl pieces, too.

The meticulous approach of De Stijl, turning the house into a 'total work of art', worked well with a sympathetic client. But it was less practical for housing schemes for the less well off. But Dutch architects of the De Stijl movement did bring their pure aesthetic to bear on mass housing projects. J.J.P. Oud, a De Stijl member who became Housing Architect for the city of Rotterdam, applied the white-walled aesthetic of simple planes and openings to workers' housing. His 1920s' Kiefhoeck and Hook of Holland estates are still widely admired.

The De Stijl movement flourished through the 1920s. Van Doesburg lectured at the Bauhaus (see pages 120–123), taking De Stijl ideas to Germany, from where they influenced architecture as Europe emerged from the First World War and the movement lasted until Van Doesburg's death in 1931. Today architects still look back to De Stijl for inspiration, and designers admire Rietveld's furniture designs – reproductions of his famous Red-Blue Chair are still produced.

the condensed idea
Clean lines, primary colours

29 Constructivism

The Russian constructivist movement flourished briefly in the 1920s and 30s. Constructivist architects produced breathtaking modern designs, often glorying in unusual and innovative structures. Although not all of these structures were actually built, they had a huge influence on architects not only in the Soviet Union, but elsewhere in Europe, too.

There are some artistic movements that, although short-lived and confined to one particular place, punch above their weight in terms of their influence. One example is constructivism, a movement that developed in Russia in the 1920s and 30s, spawned a handful of famous and innovative buildings and was eliminated as a result of changing Soviet artistic policy. But its influence lived on in the work of a constructivist group in Switzerland called ABC and in the work of the Bauhaus (see pages 120–123), and still inspires architects today.

Revolutionary beginnings Constructivism grew out of two things – an artistic avant garde that was already flourishing and asking challenging questions about art and design before the 1917 revolution and the feeling that the new post-revolutionary communist society needed new ways of looking at art and making buildings. Constructivism was not the only artistic movement that grew out of these ideas, but it was among the most important – especially for architecture.

The first great constructivist design was also the most famous. It was the Monument to the Third International designed by artist and architect Vladimir Tatlin, an extraordinary invention that only ever existed as a

timeline
1919–20
Vladimir Tatlin designs his
Monument to the Third International

large model, but which if built would have been one of the most bizarre and striking structures in the world. The monument, now widely known as Tatlin's tower, was intended to be 400 metres (1,300 ft) tall and to be stand over the River Neva in Petrograd (St Petersburg). It was to consist of a vast double spiral of girders, leaning to one side and tapering towards the top. Inside this openwork cat's cradle of metalwork was a number of suspended revolving glass rooms designed as perfect forms – a cube, a pyramid and a cylinder.

OSA

Constructivist architecture was very varied, but there were two main groupings of architects, each with its own society and defined set of views. The first was the Society of Contemporary Architects (OSA). It was led by Moisei Ginzburg and was strongly influenced by architectural developments in the West, especially by the functionalist ideas of the likes of Le Corbusier. They saw it as important in a workers' society for aesthetics to be drawn from the factory – both in terms of the functional design of factory buildings and in the appearance of mass-produced objects. OSA architects did a lot of work on the design of mass housing, basing their plans on the everyday requirements of the occupants – small bedrooms and bathrooms and larger living rooms, for example. Their buildings had many of the features common in western modernism, such as the use of long strip windows and raising building on pilotis (columns).

Down with guarding the traditions of art. Long live the Constructivist technician.

Constructivist slogan

1925	1927	1928
El Lissitsky designs his 'Cloud-hangers' project	Zuev Workers' Club is built	Rusakov Workers' Club, Moscow, is completed

Constructivist interests Tatlin's tower (left) combined a frank display of structure, a use of modern materials, an interest in pure geometry and an enthusiasm for unconventional and distorted structures, all features that fascinated the constructivists. Similar interests inspired similarly unlikely projects such as a design for a Lenin Tribune – a leaning openwork tower – by El Lissitsky, a designer now more famous as a spare and elegant abstract artist. More ostensibly practical, but equally daring, were Lissitsky's 'Cloud-hangers', towers capped with vast 'horizontal skyscrapers'. None of these was ever built, but they inspired architects looking for new ways to use materials such as steel, concrete and glass.

The constructivist projects that actually were built included Konstantin Melnikov's Rusakov Workers' Club in Moscow, which combines odd angles and forms with modernist white walls; the Zuev Workers' Club, with its glass tower; and Melnikov's own house in Moscow, again with a tower. Buildings such as these, more outré and experimental than anything being built in western Europe at the time, put Soviet Russia into the vanguard of architecture. Their designers and advocates felt that, like the abstract art that was being produced at the same time, their work represented a radical new outlook, quite appropriate for the new social system being formed under communism.

> **Construction is organization.**
> **Vladimir Tatlin**

Opponents and influences Not everyone in Russia agreed. Against those who saw the importance of new art for the new social order were those who saw the groups of artists and architects flourishing at this time as elitist and irrelevant to the people as a whole. And so, in

ASNOVA

The members of the Association of New Architecture (ASNOVA) described themselves as rationalists rather than constructivists, but they shared many of the ideas of the constructivist movement. While stressing the scientific basis of modern architecture, they also wanted their buildings to make bold, heroic gestures to inspire the people to embrace revolutionary values. The unusual structures and theatrical appearance of many ASNOVA buildings were often criticized as indulgent by the more restrained members of OSA.

1932, the proliferation of artistic groups was suppressed by the Russian leadership. Russian architecture turned away from modernism, futurism, constructivism and all the other -isms, and embraced a conservative, neo-Renaissance norm.

Some of the Russian modernists and constructivists moved to the West. El Lissitsky, for example, went to Switzerland, where he was one of the founders of the constructivist group ABC. Through this group some of the ideas of the constructivists came to the attention of other European design groups, such as the Bauhaus. Their individual take on modernism is perhaps reflected in the much later work of the deconstructivist architects of the late 20th century (see pages 196–199), who combined ideas such as the display of structure and the use of unusual angles and forms to new and provocative effect.

the condensed idea
New art for a new order

30 Bauhaus

The Bauhaus was a school of design, founded in Germany in 1919, that had a lasting influence on architecture and the design of all types of product. Its creator, Walter Gropius, aimed to marry good design with the use of machines for manufacturing and the adoption of modern materials in architecture. His methods were widely copied, and several Bauhaus designs became classics.

The Arts and Crafts movement of the late 19th century had encouraged a coming-together of all types of artists, designers and craft workers to create everything from jewellery to buildings by marrying a revival of traditional craft methods to a clear analysis of form and function. Arts and Crafts architecture, though less cluttered than the Victorian work that preceded it, still looked traditional and rooted in history. What if the ideals of good construction and close cooperation between artist, architect and artisan were focused on more modern, more industrial design?

From Werkbund to Bauhaus One answer to this was provided in Germany by an organization called the Deutsche Werkbund. Founded in 1907 in Munich, the Werkbund brought together a group of cutting-edge designers and artists who focused on designing without looking to past styles for inspiration or imitation. The group created pioneering work in design and architecture, but was not radical enough for one young architect, Walter Gropius, who wanted to move closer to industry and industrial design. In 1919, therefore, Gropius made a career move to become head of a school of arts and crafts in Weimar, which he reorganized and renamed the Bauhaus.

timeline

1919	1926
Walter Gropius founds the Bauhaus in Weimar	The new Bauhaus headquarters in Dessau, designed by Gropius, is opened

Gropius wanted to bring industry and craft closer together, to revolutionize how things are designed and made. He saw that in order to do this, he had to educate students not only in craft and design, but also in concepts such as form and colour. So he added a group of painters to the staff of the Bauhaus, men such as Paul Klee and Johannes Itten.

The introductory course Itten was especially influential because Gropius put him in charge of the *Vorkurs* – an introductory course taken by all students when they arrived at the Bauhaus – in which these key concepts of form and colour were explained. Students then went on to learn both how to make designs of objects – both for mass production and for one-off production but still in a 'machine aesthetic' – or to design buildings. Gropius championed the modern approach to architecture – exploiting both the strength and visual qualities of materials such as steel, concrete and glass and rejecting what he saw as the 'dishonest' claddings and trickeries of 19th-century architecture.

The move to Dessau When, in 1924–5, these ideas proved too radical for the backers of the Bauhaus in Weimar, Gropius moved the school to Dessau, building a striking new headquarters that, with its pale concrete walls and large windows, exemplified Bauhaus ideas. This was where some of the most famous products of Bauhaus design were created: Marcel Breuer's tubular steel and leather armchairs and Gropius's light fittings in glass and chromium, for example.

> **The Bauhaus believes the machine to be our modern medium of design and seeks to come to terms with it.**
>
> Walter Gropius, *Idea and Construction*, 1923

1926	1928	1933	1937
Marcel Breuer creates his 'Wassily' armchair of leather on a tubular steel frame	Gropius designs workers' housing for the Siemens company outside Berlin	The Bauhaus in Dessau is closed	The Bauhaus Chicago is opened under the directorship of Lázló Moholy-Nagy

The Bauhaus building

The building that Gropius designed for the Bauhaus at Dessau (below) is one of the most important of the 20th century, embodying several architectural ideas that were to be widely imitated and adapted. It was planned as a series of blocks, each with a different function – one containing teaching rooms and library, one workshops and studios, another student accommodation. These blocks were linked by a section containing a lecture hall and a bridge housing the administrative offices. This zoning, with each block expressing in its outer appearance the rooms within, was highly influential, as was the fact that the resulting plan had no 'front', just a series of wings. The freely designed spaces, the frank use of concrete and steel, and the strong straight lines were much copied, both in educational buildings and more widely.

The architectural impact of the Bauhaus also increased, as Gropius won commissions to design housing projects such as workers' housing for Siemens outside Berlin. In such schemes, as well as capitalizing on the standardization offered by using modern materials, he tried to bring air and light into his houses, to make them more attractive to live in than traditional or 19th-century dwellings.

Gropius, and the directors who succeeded him, Hannes Meyer and Ludwig Mies van der Rohe, did much to promote the values of modernist architecture through the Bauhaus, while also keeping alive the modernist version of the old Arts and Crafts ideal – that every object in the home, from crockery to curtains, should be well designed. This holistic approach is one of the most important legacies of the Bauhaus ideal.

Closure and emigration The Bauhaus was strong, but could not resist the rise of Nazism with its very different ideas about design. Hitler was interested in expressing the German character through traditional classicism, and saw little merit in modern design or its practitioners. So in 1933 the Nazis closed the school.

But in some ways this increased the influence of Bauhaus ideas. Most of the staff emigrated to the USA, where they continued to promote their type of design and where artist Lázló Moholy-Nagy briefly set up the New Bauhaus in Chicago. In the 1950s another stalwart, Swiss architect Max Bill, took Bauhaus ideas to the design school at Ulm, bringing this type of design back home once more. As a result the products of the Bauhaus, from modernist chairs to steel-and-glass buildings, are well known all over the Western world.

the condensed idea
Design for the machine age

31 The International Style

The International Style was the name chosen to describe the modernist architecture of the 1920s and early 30s, when the work of architects such as Mies van der Rohe, Walter Gropius and Le Corbusier was exhibited in New York in 1932. Their architecture of free planning and their aesthetic of functionalism became highly influential and seemed to sum up the ideals of modern architects in the decades before and after the Second World War.

By the end of the 1920s the most adventurous architects had evolved a way of building that became symbolic of what was progressive and new in 20th-century design. Modern communications meant that this way of building was international – buildings in California could look similar to those in Europe or Australia. It is not surprising that this architecture became known as the International Style.

The MoMA exhibition The most famous early use of the term 'International Style' was in 1932, when the writer Henry-Russell Hitchcock and architect Philip Johnson curated the International Exhibition of Modern Architecture at New York's Museum of Modern Art (MoMA). The book they produced to accompany the exhibition was called *The International Style*.

timeline

1923

Le Corbusier publishes *Vers Une Architecture* (*Towards An Architecture*, also translated as *Towards a New Architecture*), which includes an outline of his 'five points'

1924

J.J.P. Oud begins to work on workers' housing projects in the Hook of Holland

Hitchcock and Johnson's exhibition contained many of the key buildings of the 1920s: villas in France designed by Le Corbusier, the German Bauhaus designed by Walter Gropius, houses in Holland by J.J.P. Oud and buildings by Erich Mendelsohn and Mies van der Rohe. In some ways these structures were very diverse – Oud's workers' houses, for example, looked very different from a large department store by Mendelsohn. But seen together, several key features emerged.

Five points of a new architecture

Le Corbusier outlined five key points that were characteristic of the new architecture as he saw it, exemplified in his Villa Savoye (below).

- Raising the building on pilotis, so that the main structure seems to 'float' above the ground.
- The provision of a roof garden.
- The 'free plan'. In a free plan, and with the structure held up by the pilotis, rooms and interior spaces could be arranged as function dictated, without the need to include structural walls.
- The 'free façade'. With rooms arranged at will, the façade could take whatever form function dictated. Walls did not need to be structural because the pilotis carried the weight of floors and roof.
- The use of strip windows to admit plenty of light.

1929
Mies van der Rohe's German Pavilion is a major element in the Barcelona Exposition, Spain

1930
Erich Mendelsohn's Schocken Department Store, Chemnitz, Germany, is built

1931
Le Corbusier's Villa Savoye is built in Poissy, Paris

1932
Henry-Russell Hitchcock and architect Philip Johnson put on the International Exhibition of Modern Architecture at New York's Museum of Modern Art

Features of the style Key features included the use of concrete, steel and glass, the rejection of ornament, asymmetry and truth to materials. International Style buildings also tended to show an interest in volume rather than mass. In other words, in rejecting thick, load-bearing walls the buildings felt light and transparent, and a far cry from the massive qualities of a castle or an Arts and Crafts house. But the volumes, the spaces inside the building, were meticulously worked out and artfully defined by partition walls, screens and windows.

This quality of lightness and transparency was especially powerful. Architects exploited the way in which steel and concrete structures could be held above the ground on pillars (or 'pilotis' as they became known), and the way in which cantilevered structures could make upper stories seem to float in space. Generous windows enhanced this effect of lightness, too.

These buildings could also be international in another way. Architects such as Walter Gropius were keen to embrace the possibilities of machine-made components. At the Bauhaus (see pages 120–123), students learned to make high-quality designs that could be mass produced. Factory-made components of a building, from girders to door handles, could be reproduced in any place where the right production facilities existed, so buildings were no longer tied to local traditions, materials and construction techniques.

Functionalism Modernist architecture was wedded to the notion that 'form follows function', so architects were encouraged to work 'outwards' from the specific requirements of a building's users, creating the spaces that would best meet these needs. The exterior appearance of the building – its shape, the arrangement of the façades and so on –

❝... architecture is a social art related to the life of the people it serves, not an academic exercise in applied ornament.❞

J.M. Richards, *An Introduction to Modern Architecture*

Planning on a grid

When working according to the 'five points', architects laid out the pilotis at regular intervals, to form a structural grid. This was just one example of grid planning, a system that was used widely by 20th-century architects. This type of planning could be a structural device – a way of enabling builders to use standard components, such as wall panels of the same size – or simply a discipline to create an ordered plan. Grid planning was frequently used for industrial buildings so that concrete frameworks and similar items could be made to standard sizes and building became a task of assembling components.

would follow on from this, which is why modernist buildings are often asymmetrical.

However, architects of the calibre of Le Corbusier and Mies van der Rohe were highly visually aware, and sought to make the exteriors of their buildings carefully composed and balanced, even when they were not symmetrical. This fact gives many modernist buildings, such as Le Corbusier's villas, a studied elegance.

An attractive package By ignoring styles such as expressionism (see pages 108–111) and the works of major individual (and individualist) architects, such as Frank Lloyd Wright, Hitchcock and Johnson defined a style of modern architecture. It was an attractive package and, because it included the work of architects of renown, it inspired many followers. The fact that its ideas could be wrapped in pithy, memorable phrases – such as 'form follows function' and Le Corbusier's 'a house is a machine for living in' – made it accessible and easy to publicize, too. As a result, the International Style was influential in the 1930s and remained so after the Second World War.

the condensed idea
Modernism goes global

32 Minimalism

One of the most familiar interior design styles of recent decades is minimalism – plain walls, surfaces uninterrupted by ornament or mouldings, zero clutter. Fashionable as it is, minimalism goes back a long way – to the work of the modernist architects of the 1920s and their attempts to forge new ways of building without looking back to the past.

The legacy of the mid 19th century was a powerful one in architecture and design. It was the era of the Gothic revival, of decoration richly detailed, of rooms made dark with heavy drapes, of a world of intricate clutter. By the beginning of the 20th century architects had tried various ways of breaking free and starting afresh – the Arts and Crafts revival and Art Nouveau had both tried to make a new start. The various types of modernism – Bauhaus, De Stijl, the International Style – made more radical breaks with the past. Minimalism was one form of modern design that broke more radically than the rest.

The German architect Ludwig Mies van der Rohe made his name in the mid 1920s for his use of industrial materials. His apartment block at the Weissenhof Siedlung (a permanent exhibition of buildings by the prominent modernist architects of the time) was the first such block in Europe to have a steel frame. The apartments looked purposeful and modern, and were designed with careful logic.

The Barcelona Pavilion But in the following years Mies turned in a new direction. The building with which he made this turn was the German Pavilion he designed for the Barcelona International

timeline

1929

Barcelona Pavilion designed by Mies van der Rohe, constructed; the pavilion was demolished but reconstructed in 1992

1946–51

Mies van der Rohe's Farnsworth House, Plano, Illinois, designed

Exhibition in 1929. This is a building that was designed to be virtually empty – an abstract collection of spaces bounded – or partly bounded – by walls in rich materials (green marble and onyx) and supported by columns clad in chrome. One space was dominated by a pool in which

The I-beam

A key component of metal-framed buildings is the I-beam – a rolled-steel joist with a cross-section like a capital letter I that was prized for its strength and connectivity. In most buildings these beams are hidden, but when he built the Farnsworth House (below),

Mies used exposed I-beams for the main structure, specifying a high-quality white finish on their surfaces to bring out their elegance. The treatment of the I-beams on the Farnsworth House is a good example of the minimalist attention to surface details.

1949	1981	1983	1988
Philip Johnson's house, New Canaan, Connecticut, built	Tadao Ando's Koshino House, Hyogo, completed	Glenn Murcutt's Ball-Eastaway House, Glenorie, NSW, completed	Tadao Ando's Church on the Water, Tomamu, completed

'Less is more.'

Ludwig Mies van der Rohe

stood a statue of a female nude; another space was furnished with a few of Mies's metal-framed Barcelona chairs; one section of floor was carpeted in black; one window was covered with a red curtain. And that was all.

The Barcelona Pavilion was a special case, a building meant as a beautiful object in an exhibition. The visitor could revel in the rich surfaces, the reflected light from the pool, the elegance of it all, and move on. But what would happen if you designed a functional building in this way? Mies's answer was the Tugendhat House, Brno, Czech Republic, which he built along similar lines to the Pavilion in 1930. But the ultimate answer came 20 years later, when he designed a house for Dr Edith Farnsworth in Plano, Illinois.

The minimalist house The Farnsworth House is raised above the ground on steel columns that also support the flat roof. The outside 'skin' of the building is glass – there are no walls in the conventional sense of the word. The interior is one large space broken only by a long rectangular service core containing the bathrooms and kitchen.

Mies's associate Philip Johnson was one of those who followed in the master's footsteps. Johnson's own house at New Canaan, Connecticut, was planned on similar lines except that, unlike the Farnsworth House, it sits close to the ground on a low plinth and has a circular bathroom core.

Neither the Farnsworth nor the Johnson house has the same lavish use of materials seen in the Barcelona Pavilion. The Farnsworth residence did maintain hints of richness, however, with teak woodwork, a floor of travertine and silk curtains. But the emphasis in both houses is on the connection with the surrounding landscape and on the relentless lack of anything normally thought of as architecture. No other buildings live up so completely to the minimalist ideal.

Buildings such as this need forgiving clients. Edith Farnsworth found it impossible to live in her house, which was like an oven in summer. It seemed that minimalist architecture had no future after this. Yet the purity of the idea has haunted architects and designers. Its influence is felt in countless banks of white kitchen cupboards and in visually impoverished interior makeovers.

Recent minimalism

The influence of Minimalism has continued through the 1970s to today. The Japanese architect Tadao Ando builds poetic concrete structures that are severely minimalist. But in their sensitive handling of light and their meticulous detailing they are more humane than the work of Mies. Ando's Koshino House, Hyogo, and his Church on the Water, Tomamu, and many of his other buildings, are object lessons in concrete minimalism.

The Australian architect Glenn Murcutt also designs minimalist houses, generously glazed and with much use of steel and corrugated iron, some of them almost as open to their surroundings as the Farnsworth House. But by playing close attention to ventilation and light, and by careful integration of house and surroundings, Murcutt makes his houses popular with their owners and kind to the environment. By finding in Minimalism what works, architects such as Ando and Murcutt have taken architecture in exciting new directions.

the condensed idea
Keep it simple

33 Art Deco

In the 1920s a number of French designers promoted a style that made ornament modern. They turned their backs on traditional classical and Gothic forms of architectural decoration, drawing inspiration from sources as distant as ancient Egypt to combine vivid colour and pattern with modern lines. The result was Art Deco, and it had a huge impact in the period between the two world wars.

In the modern architecture of the 1920s and 1930s the most ubiquitous way of working was what became known as the International Style (see pages 124–7) or International Modernism – the way of building in which form was said to follow function, materials (concrete, steel and glass) were enjoyed for their intrinsic qualities and ornament was virtually banished. But there was also a contrary tendency, a style of architecture and decoration in which modern materials were used in conjunction with bold and often exotic geometric ornament. This style has come to be known as Art Deco.

A formative exhibition Art Deco began in France under the auspices of a group of French artists and designers called the Société des artistes décorateurs. In 1925 the society organized an exhibition in Paris, the *Exposition Internationale des Arts Décoratifs et Industriels Modernes*. This exhibition included a range of designs and styles – Russian constructivism was represented, for example, as were the pared-down designs of men such as Le Corbusier, which were key to International Modernism. But at the exhibition's heart was a variety of highly decorative, luxury objects – the items that first defined the Art

timeline

1925	1930
The *Exposition Internationale des Arts Décoratifs et Industriels Modernes* is held in Paris	Chrysler Building, New York, is completed

Deco style – the name of which derives from the words *Arts Décoratifs* in the exhibition title.

Art Deco style was defined by the decoration used on the object and this had an eclectic range of sources: a type of stylized, streamlined classicism; the use of geometrical patterns to produce crystal-like shapes; decorative motifs drawn from ancient Egyptian, Aztec and African art; and the use of splashes of bright colour or rich gilding in combination with pale backgrounds. Stylized fountains, sunbursts and lightning flashes were popular ornamental patterns; polished steel and aluminium and inlaid woods were prominent materials.

From decoration to architecture Art Deco provides a popular style for a host of decorative items from pottery and table lamps to statuettes, often featuring glamorous women – clothed or naked – on striking geometrical bases. The style also caught on in architecture in the 1920s and 1930s. Its decorative flair made it attractive for houses, hotels and commercial buildings – the two most famous early New York skyscrapers – the Empire State and Chrysler buildings – are both examples of Art Deco.

Industrialists liked to use the style for their factories, sensing that the decorative style, which could transfer with ease from package design to architecture, enabled them to display their brand on a large scale. Cinema owners, too, found Art Deco, with its strong lines and decorative flair, ideal for their buildings.

❝Cosmetic Deco and moderne façades brought a face-lift to Main Street America . . .❞

Stephen Sennott, *Encyclopedia of Twentieth-Century Architecture*

1931
Empire State Building, New York, is opened

1932
Radio City Music Hall, Rockefeller Center, New York, is opened

1934
The Chrysler Airflow is introduced and has a strong influence on streamlining in design

Streamline moderne

The streamline moderne style is a cousin of Art Deco that emerged in the 1930s. Inspired in part by the long, low, curvaceous lines of streamlined automobiles such as the 1930s Chrysler Airflow, it applied the aesthetics of streamlining to buildings. Streamline moderne buildings often have a horizontal, ground-hugging emphasis. They make prominent use of horizontal accents, such as long strips of windows – often metal-framed with plenty of horizontal glazing bars – and balconies with long rails like those on ocean liners. Unlike Art Deco buildings, which are all sharp angles and crystalline forms, streamline moderne buildings also incorporate curves – round, porthole-like windows, circular electric light fittings and curving corners; sometimes even bay or end windows that turn the corner with a curved pane of glass.

Deco around the world And Art Deco did spread widely around the world. Cities that were being aggressively developed in the 1930s were hotbeds of the style – there are still many Art Deco buildings in Miami, Havana, Cuba, and the larger towns of Indonesia. And the town of Napier, New Zealand, severely damaged in an earthquake in 1931, was largely rebuilt in the style. Its concentration of Art Deco buildings is still famous.

A popular style Thanks to the luxurious cinemas and hotels Art Deco had a popular following. But it was rather frowned on by many architects, who preferred the more rigorous 'form follows function' aesthetic of International Modernism. For modernist architects and many architectural critics, Art Deco was an ephemeral style, fit more for ashtrays and statuettes than for buildings. But what put an end to the fashion for Art Deco was the beginning of the Second World War, which in 1939 imposed a virtual stop on building in many parts of the world.

Naming the style

The term Art Deco is now very familiar. It comes from the title of the 1925 Paris exhibition, the *Exposition Internationale des Arts Décoratifs et Industriels Modernes*, that introduced the style. But the term was not much used when the style was fashionable – people originally referred to it as the *Style Moderne,* or simply as *Moderne*. In the 1960s there was a revival of interest in the style, and writer and critic Bevis Hillier published a book *Art Deco of the 20s and 30s,* which popularized this name, leaving the term *Moderne* for use in connection with the streamlined, automobile-inspired style that developed shortly after Art Deco itself.

After the war ended, and planners and architects began to begin the vast rebuilding programmes that were needed, they looked to the more sober modernist style. Art Deco survived in the interior decorations schemes of a few new restaurants and department stores, but was mostly seen as a memory of earlier, more frivolous times.

the condensed idea
Making ornament modern

34 Organic architecture

For thousands of years writers on architecture have compared the creations of builders and architecture to the natural world. The great American architect Frank Lloyd Wright made his entire career in what he called Organic architecture. His houses were sensitive to site, carefully related to their gardens and outstanding in their use of materials.

Wright grew up in the 19th century under the influence of the great American architect Louis Sullivan, for whom he worked for a while, and the English Arts and Crafts movement. But his greatest buildings were designed in the 20th century, during a long career that lasted until the architect's death in 1959.

During this long working life Wright developed the theory and practice of Organic architecture, exploring the way in which architect and environment interact. This way of building embraced the Arts and Crafts ideals of truth to materials – Wright liked natural materials and hated covering wood or stone surfaces with coloured paint or plaster.

The four elements However, Wright's desire to bring his buildings closer to nature went deeper than this. Harking back to the science of the ancient world, he liked the idea that the cosmos was made up of the four elements – earth, air, fire and water. So in many houses by Wright, all of these elements play their part.

timeline

1909
Robie House, Chicago, one of the greatest Prairie Houses, is designed

Prairie Houses

Wright called many of his larger houses Prairie Houses. These were low-slung structures, often with cross-shaped or pinwheel plans, that sprawled across their sites. Wright believed that this type of design produced a house that was very close to the earth and fitting for the open spaces of the American Midwest – even though some of these buildings, like Robie House (below), were in the suburbs of Chicago.

Earth is present in exposed brickwork, inside and out. The brickwork in many of Wright's houses is beautifully crafted, with delicate, slender bricks used in archways around openings and fireplaces.

Air is present because a typical Organic house has many doors and French windows opening into the garden and on to terraces and balconies. The owners of a house by Wright are invited to spend as much of their lives as possible in the airy, semi-outdoor spaces of these terraces, which open off living rooms, bedrooms, even studies.

1936	**1939**	**1944**
Fallingwater, Wright's house over a waterfall at Bear Run, Pennsylvania	Wright is at work on several of his best Usonian Houses	Wright pioneers earth-sheltered building in the Jacobs House, Middleton, Wisconsin

> **❛Any building for humane purposes should be an elemental, sympathetic feature of the ground.❜**
>
> **Frank Lloyd Wright, quoted in William J.R. Curtis,**
> *Modern Architecture Since 1900*

Fire was a vital element for Wright. He saw the hearth as the symbolic and literal centre of the home, and many of his houses are planned around a central fireplace. Throughout his life Wright devised different ways of building houses around central hearths, drawing residents towards the warmth and inviting light of the fire.

Water is less easy to bring into a house in a visible way, but Wright sometimes managed it. His most famous house, Fallingwater, at Bear Run, Pennsylvania, is built over a waterfall – the sound of the torrent is ever present. Another house has a small water channel running through the floor and around the hearth, as if the fire is protected by a miniature moat. And a third has a circular pool half inside and half outside the main living room.

House and landscape As will be clear from his inclusion of air in the four elements, Wright was also insistent on the close relationship between inside and outside, house and garden. Like an Arts and Crafts architect, he drew up plans that included the garden, sometimes linking building and landscaping with structures such as terraces and pergolas. The masonry of balconies often includes planters, bringing the green world of the garden right up to the house.

Usonian Houses

Wright developed the idea of the Usonian House for clients who could not afford his larger designs. The name (derived from 'US') again signals a specifically American approach. The houses are built with natural materials, including a great deal of wood, use space economically and are simply constructed. Like all Wright's buildings, they are tailored carefully to their sites.

Wright claimed that he wanted his houses to have minimal impact on the landscape. He said that a house should not be placed 'on' a hill, but should be 'of' the hill – in other words, that it should form an organic part of the landscape, not look like something imported from outside.

Wright did not always succeed in this. Some of his buildings have such a strong presence that, for all their use of natural materials and their careful placing, they seem more like landmarks than buildings truly 'of' their environment. Some of his small houses, wooden-sided, low-slung buildings for middle-income Americans, are more successful in this regard. And the architect's own two large houses, Taliesin in Wisconsin and Taliesin West in Arizona, also seem to emerge from their setting – Taliesin from its hillside and Taliesin West, with its vast chunks of local rock, from the Arizona desert nearby.

Wright's ideas about organic architecture have proved increasingly popular with architects who want to minimize the environmental impact of their structures while producing buildings that are both attractive and sustainable. Many of these designers, as well as drawing influence from Wright's ideas, are inspired by the vernacular tradition in which for centuries local builders have used local materials to design in locally distinctive and environmentally appropriate ways.

To combine energy efficiency and a low impact on the landscape, some Organic architects have also used earth-sheltered building, in which the structure is partly buried underground (see page 194). So beginning with the ideas of pioneers such as Frank Lloyd Wright, architects today have taken Organic architecture in new directions, producing beautiful and inspiring buildings that are also sensitive to the needs of both client and planet.

the condensed idea
Building and site in harmony

35 Dymaxion design

Richard Buckminster Fuller combined the roles of engineer, inventor and architect to produce a number of innovative designs, the most famous of which were variations on the geodesic dome. Fuller liked the dome because it could cover so much space with so little material, an economy of means that was summed up by the term 'Dymaxion', which Fuller used to describe most of his designs.

Buckminster Fuller was an American engineer who had a gift for looking at the world in a different way from most other people. He produced a series of designs – for houses, a bathroom, a car, a world map projection and, most famously, various geodesic domes – that proved interesting and inspiring to generations of architects and designers, although, with the exception of the domes, they mostly failed to make it past the prototype stage. Fuller also wrote copiously, and came up with a number of memorable terms to describe his work and ideas.

Dynamic maximum tension Dymaxion was one of Fuller's favourite terms, although it does not seem to have been invented by him, but by an advertising man looking for a way of describing one of Fuller's house designs. It was derived by combining the words dynamic, maximum and tension.

timeline

1930
Model of the hexagonal Dymaxion House shown at the Chicago Arts Club

1933
First Dymaxion Car prototype is constructed

For Fuller it also contained the idea that his designs would make the maximum use of the available energy – he was a pioneer environmentalist who thought that we would all be using renewable energy within his lifetime (he died in 1983). So the term Dymaxion summed up his key interests and, at the same time, reminded people that his designs, although very diverse, were the products of one mind.

Dymaxion houses Fuller's first famous project was the Dymaxion House of the late 1920s. It was intended to provide a cheap and effective dwelling that could be erected easily; he also wanted the structure to be light in weight so that it could be transported anywhere with minimal cost. The most refined form of the design was a curious hexagonal structure hung from a central mast. A 10-storey Dymaxion skyscraper was also proposed and a model of the house exhibited.

Fuller proposed the radical use of materials in his house designs – the artificial substance Casein for walls, ceilings and bathroom fittings; rubber floors; aluminium alloy for various structural elements. He claimed that the whole structure would cost less than one-fifth of the cost of the average conventional new home.

But the Dymaxion House was too unconventional to catch on, as was its successor – the so-called Wichita House of the 1940s. This was a stunning, circular, metal-roofed design meant to be built by the American aircraft industry and incorporating such innovations as closets with revolving shelves, Dymaxion bathrooms and a clever air-circulating system driven by the wind. Again, it was light in weight,

> **We have come to the realization that we areich in an all-dynamic universe.**
>
> Richard Buckminster Fuller, *Preview of Building*

1945	1948	1958	1967
Prototype of the circular Wichita House is built	Fuller begins to teach a design class at Black Mountain College, where he starts work on geodesic domes	Union Tank Car repair shop dome at Baton Rouge, Louisiana, is constructed	US Pavilion at the Montreal Exhibition is constructed in the form of a large geodesic dome

easily shipped and could be assembled in a day by a team of six. The house should have been a success, but Fuller's company folded because of disputes among directors.

The ill-fated car A similar fate accompanied the Dymaxion car – a bizarre three-wheeled vehicle with many innovative features, but stability problems that led to a fatal accident. Fuller's ideas seemed destined to fail and, like other unsuccessful architects and designers before and since, he took up a teaching post.

Space frames

The geodesic dome is a space-frame structure. This is a type of design that encloses space by means of a structure made up of many interconnecting elements that act together as a unity. Space frames can be supported at almost any of the points where the elements connect and they are ideal for spanning large volumes of space with few, or no, columns. Space frames do not have to be dome-shaped. They may be made up of pyramids, hexagons or several other geometric shapes.

Geodesic domes Fuller taught at the whacky, but influential, Black Mountain College, North Carolina. Here he had his students build geodesic domes, the one type of structure that brought Fuller lasting success. A geodesic dome is a structure made up of lightweight rods in hexagons (or other geometrical figures) that join together to make a sphere or hemisphere. Fuller did not invent the geodesic dome, but it appealed to him because it is a very lightweight, low-energy type of structure – you can cover a huge volume of space with a minimum of material using a geodesic dome.

Fuller's first experiment with a dome made from recycled Venetian blind parts was a failure. It collapsed because the blind slats were not stiff enough. But soon he had worked out how to build domes from all types of materials – wood, bamboo, aluminium, steel and concrete. Fuller saw that a small geodesic dome could form a house, but geodesic domes could also be made much bigger – to accommodate factories or exhibition halls. And it was such vast domes that became Fuller's most famous legacy.

Although several of Fuller's first domes were built for the American military, the dome that brought this type of building into the public eye was the Ford Rotunda roof, a 28-metre (92-ft) diameter structure for the Ford Motor Company's site at Dearborn, Michigan. Larger and more impressive was one of two domes for the Union Tank Car Company. At Baton Rouge, Louisiana, this monster dome was 116 metres (380 ft) across and, at the time, was the largest clear-span enclosure in the world.

Domes such as these gave Fuller a lasting importance as a designer. His lateral thinking, ecological values and openness to new materials have made him widely admired by many architects and engineers ever since.

the condensed idea
Dynamic maximum tension

36 Segregated planning

Mass car ownership and the increased traffic it brought posed a major challenge to architects and planners. For decades, the obvious solution seemed to be to segregate pedestrians and traffic to make people safer and more comfortable and to allow cars to move quickly. But taken to its logical conclusion in the 1950s and 1960s, the idea proved a disastrous failure.

The garden city movement of the late 19th century is remembered for the way it encouraged the greening of the city (see pages 96–99). But another major part of the garden city idea was zoning – each part of the city had a specific purpose (housing, shopping, industry, parks and so on) and the zones were linked by a carefully planned network of major and minor roads.

Radburn planning The city planners of the 20th century took this idea of zoning still further, and applied it not only to the functions of the parts of the town, but also to the transport arteries. The most famous pioneering example of this was the town of Radburn, New Jersey, which was founded in 1929 with a plan specifically tailored to the age of motor transport.

For Radburn's planners the key was to separate cars and pedestrians. They developed a system of pedestrian paths and used bridges and underpasses to allow these to cross the motor roads. The aim was to

timeline
1929
Radburn, New Jersey, founded as a 'town for the motor age'

increase pedestrian safety and also to keep traffic flowing and the town seemed to answer for the first time the question of how urban centres could deal with the car.

Radburn set other trends in planning, too. The residential areas of the town were laid out in 'super blocks', each of which contained a network of culs-de-sac that gave streets a feeling of seclusion and privacy. In addition, local access roads were separated form the main through routes to help the traffic flow and make navigation easier.

A delayed reaction This type of planning was inspiring, and had Radburn not been founded in a time of economic depression, might have caught on quickly. As it was, the influence of Radburn came late, but spread more widely. Some of its principles – especially the hierarchy of roads and pedestrian routes – were adopted by the modernist group CIAM, and they began to appear in modernist plans after the Second World War. Chandigarh, the capital of the Punjab, planned by Albert Mayer, Matthew Nowicki and Le Corbusier, was a famous example.

So, promoted by modernist architects and in response to increasing car ownership and goods traffic, segregated planning became commonplace in the 1950s and 1960s. It seemed logical and safe to separate pedestrians and cars, and architects saw opportunities to make new types of buildings based on the idea of keeping cars and pedestrians separate.

> **❝. . . claustrophobic walk-ups or corridors were rejected in favour of 12ft-wide "streets in the sky" . . . The architects thought they had solved the problems of modernist housing.❞**
>
> **Owen Hatherley**, writing in the *Guardian*

1950	**1961**	**1967**
After the death of architect Matthew Nowicki, Le Corbusier is brought in to plan Chandigarh and design major buildings in the city	Park Hill Estate, Sheffield, designed by Jack Lynn and Ivor Smith in the brutalist style, is completed	London's Queen Elizabeth Hall is opened, with its surrounding complex of concrete walkways

Enter the walkway The result was a multitude of large building projects – from housing schemes to public buildings – in which access was via pedestrian walkways. Such schemes seemed exciting, because they offered safe, traffic-free routes as well as interesting new urban spaces in which pedestrians could walk, gather, shop and even sit at café tables, in comfort. Away from traffic noise and fumes, life would be easier. And separate access roads to garages and parking spaces were provided, usually at the back of the buildings out of sight and earshot of all the pedestrian activity.

The shopping mall

This type of building in which pedestrians are sheltered in comfort and cars are parked conveniently nearby has flourished commercially in the last 50 years. But although shopping malls have their architectural ancestry in the elegant arcades and markets of the 19th century, most are architecturally undistinguished. In addition they have been widely criticized for attracting stores and shoppers away from town centres, leading to economic decline in some inner cities.

Combined with the bright new world of concrete-and-glass architecture that was the fashion in the post-war period, this type of planning seemed to offer a new utopia – a world in which people could benefit from mass car ownership without being overwhelmed by it. It also seemed to offer a way of 'humanizing' monolithic housing blocks by providing pedestrian 'streets in the sky', where people could meet and talk as they walked to their front doors.

Unforeseen consequences Mostly, however, the concept did not work. Streets in the sky became the haunt of muggers and raised walkways were too often bleak and windswept. Concrete buildings turned from shining white to dirty, weathered grey. Even high-profile schemes, such as the pedestrian walkways giving access to the arts venues on London's South Bank, looked lacklustre a few years after construction.

In many cases there was only one solution to the toxic combination of poorly maintained concrete buildings and discredited segregated planning: demolish the lot and start again. So by the 1990s, many 1960s' blocks and walkways had been reduced to rubble, having had a far shorter life than the 19th-century terraced houses that many of them had replaced.

Conserve or demolish?

Segregated planning has a long history, and early examples of pedestrian walkways and bridges like the covered bridge in Lewisburg, West Virginia (below), are now valued by conservationists. Some of the housing schemes of the 1960s are now controversial because they are seen by some architects and critics as representing the best of 1960s' architecture, although they have deteriorated structurally and often socially. This leaves planners in a dilemma: do they give permission for demolition or spend vast amounts of money restoring buildings that did not work the first time around? At the huge Park Hill estate in Sheffield, a

listed brutalist scheme completed in 1961 with 'streets in the sky', a restoration is underway. The Robin Hood Gardens estate (completed in 1972) in East London, by contrast, has not been listed and is threatened with demolition.

the condensed idea
Separate people and traffic

37 Heritage

The way we have looked at historical buildings has changed greatly over the past 150 years. From being all but ignored by the authorities, historic architecture became a central part of our 'heritage' in a movement that led to much more rigorous preservation, but which was also sometimes connected to a false or nostalgic view of the past.

Organizations such as the SPAB (see pages 84–87) did ground-breaking work, showing the best ways to repair and maintain old buildings. But these were voluntary organizations – it was still up to owners to carry works out in the best way. Not all of them did this, and throughout the 19th and early 20th centuries many important old buildings in Britain and in other countries were demolished.

Protection by law One solution was to introduce legal protection for important monuments or buildings. Greece was a pioneer in this area. The country was the first to pass a law to protect ancient monuments, in 1834. The Danes followed suit and, in the 19th century, Germany, Holland, Italy, Sweden and the USA also started to bring in legislation to protect important historical structures. France, too, long after Victor Hugo's cry to 'still the hammer that is mutilating the face of the country', passed a Historical Monuments Act in 1887.

Britain as well acquired an Ancient Monuments Act in the 1880s. Its remit, however, was quite restricted – to such monuments as earthworks, burial mounds, stone circles, and ruined abbeys.

timeline

1894
First meeting of the English National Trust takes place

1947
British Parliament makes the listing of historic buildings a statutory duty of government

Under threat In 1893 Britain responded to appeals to preserve and protect both ancient buildings and natural scenery through another voluntary body – the National Trust. Set up to acquire and maintain 'places of interest or beauty', it concentrated at first on landscape and scenery, but later acquired many historic buildings and showed the way to similar organizations in other parts of the world.

Heritage and war Meanwhile the huge economic changes in the early 20th century had a profound impact on old buildings. After the First World War, the owners of many historic houses could no longer afford to run them, and hundreds were demolished. By the eve of the Second World War, however, many were mourning the loss of those buildings, and regretting that much of Britain's architectural heritage had been thrown away.

The term 'heritage' began to become widespread at this time and, when war came, people saw themselves as defending from further destruction the historical birthright of Britain. Heritage became key to national identity – a fact that was highlighted in books such as the 'Face of Britain' (on regions of Britain) and 'British Heritage' series published by Batsford. Other publications, such as the Shell Guides to English counties, did more to present heritage to a wider public.

> **The notion of "heritage" has been broadened and indeed transformed to take in not only the ivied church and village green but also the terraced street, the railway cottages, the covered market and even the city slum . . .**
>
> Raphael Samuel, *Theatres of Memory*

1949
The National Trust for Historic Preservation is created in the USA

1984
A new body, English Heritage, takes over sites previously managed by the government's Ministry of Works and acts as the government's statutory adviser on Heritage

Listing buildings Wartime also saw the birth of Britain's building listing system, in which historic buildings are graded, listed and protected by law. The system did not come soon enough to save yet more country houses demolished in the 1950s, but has since provided an effective way of protecting historic and architecturally important buildings. The growth of still more voluntary groups – local civic societies and national specialist groups, such as the Georgian Group and Victorian Society, for example – did more for the cause of old buildings. English Heritage, the government quango set up both to advise government on conservation matters and act as custodian of many state-owned sites, made a major contribution, too.

Listed buildings

In 1940s Britain buildings inspectors set out to make the first lists of the country's important and historic buildings. So that they knew which structures to list for protection, they followed a series of guidelines about the types of buildings that were of interest.

- Major examples of the work of specific architects.
- Buildings that typify a specific style of architecture.
- Structures that are interesting because they have altered organically over the years, displaying a hotchpotch of styles.
- Follies and other 'bizarre buildings'.
- Structures that evoke the lives of past generations, including important industrial sites.
- Buildings associated with a particular historical figure.
- Buildings that, while not important in themselves, form part of a major historical group of structures.

The rise of nostalgia But there was another side to the preservation movement, sometimes seen as less beneficial. The work of conservationists, the National Trust, country house owners throwing open their doors and setting up wildlife parks in their grounds, of historically minded entrepreneurs and canny travel companies also turned heritage into an industry. Feeding on a nostalgia for a partly fictional past, it fed visitors a partial view of history.

Nostalgia ruled, and critics mourned the fact that Britain and other countries were in danger of turning into historic theme parks. During a period when manufacturing industries in Western Europe were closing or moving to Asia, it seemed to some that making money from a false image of a rosy past was no substitute for an economy that had once produced real goods. Others, including the cultural critic Robert Hewison, pointed to the deadening effect on culture that nostalgia could have.

A changing focus One corrective to this nostalgia was a welcome willingness to change the focus of history. English Heritage and the National Trust increasingly preserved ordinary buildings, told the stories of staff and servants when they opened big houses to the public and displayed the findings of industrial archaeologists about mines, mills and factory life.

These more recent changes have led many people to be more questioning about what the heritage industry and the buildings in its care tell us. And visitors are now better informed about the architecture of the past and its social setting than ever. But neither the nostalgia, nor the proliferation of heritage 'products', from souvenir shops to nostalgia, has entirely gone away.

the condensed idea
Looking back to the past

38 Brutalism

The style known as brutalism was a bold, distinctive version of modernism that became popular in the 1960s. Typified by extensive use of concrete and strong, block-like forms, it was used widely in many types of large buildings, from university campuses to housing schemes. Criticized by many for their grim inhumanity, the brutalist buildings are still admired by numerous architects and conservationists.

By the end of the Second World War modernist architecture had developed in various ways and through various channels, from the drama of Russian constructivism to the pure machine aesthetic of the Bauhaus. Reconstruction after the war brought huge opportunities for architects, and the 1950s and 1960s saw the construction of more modernist concrete buildings than the interwar years when modernism developed.

Blocks and concrete Several of the most famous early modernists, such as Le Corbusier and Ludwig Mies van der Rohe, were still active, and Le Corbusier in particular was designing buildings that excited post-war architects. Among his projects that became especially famous were his *Unité d'Habitation*, a vast apartment block in Marseilles that included shops, a crèche and other facilities, and his buildings for Chandigarh, the new capital of the Punjab in India.

One thing that impressed about these buildings was their marked, rectilinear geometry and strong block-like appearance. In structures such as the High Court at Chandigarh, large overhanging concrete roofs,

timeline

1933	1947–52	1958–63
CIAM issues its Athens Charter	Le Corbusier's *Unité d'Habitation,* Marseilles, built	Yale University Art and Architecture Building, designed by Paul Rudolph, constructed

CIAM

CIAM (*les Congrès Internationaux d'Architecture Moderne*) was an international body providing a forum for architects to discuss their art. It began in the 1920s and its conferences became a key meeting place for modernist architects. Heavily influenced by the ideas of Le Corbusier, CIAM promoted architecture based on function and on social and economic factors. It thus played a key role in promoting modernism in its early decades. CIAM also had a strong influence on the brutalist generation through the 1933 Athens Charter. This advocated high-rise apartment blocks with green spaces around them and zoned cities, with green areas between zones devoted to housing, work, recreation and transport.

projecting side walls of concrete and rows of recessed windows produced this blocky effect, which was enhanced by the strong Indian sunlight.

Another feature of this architect's work in this period was his way of using poured concrete. The material was formed in wooden moulds, and when the timber was removed the patterns of the grain were left exposed on the surface of the concrete. Le Corbusier called this material *béton brut* ('raw concrete').

Modern grandeur This combination of *béton brut* and a block-like design seemed to offer a way of using the materials of modernism to design buildings on a large scale, to create a sense of grandeur in a modern idiom. Such buildings could be imposing and dramatic, while also giving the surface of the concrete visual interest. The style seemed well suited to the type of apartment blocks, office towers, shopping centres and multistorey car parks that were needed in reconstructed Europe. It also suited university campuses in both Europe and America.

1966
Rayner Banham publishes *The New Brutalism*

1967
The Hayward Gallery and Queen Elizabeth Hall on London's South Bank are designed by the LCC Architects Department

1968–72
Robin Hood Gardens housing scheme, London, designed by the Smithsons, constructed

> **"The warehouse aesthetic" [was] a very fair description of what The New Brutalism stood for in its first phase.**
>
> Rayner Banham, *'The New Brutalism' in* A Critic Writes: Selected Essays

Prominent exponents of the style included the British husband-and-wife team Alison and Peter Smithson, Ernö Goldfinger, Sir Denys Lasdun, William Meyer, the Scottish firm of Gillespie, Kidd & Coia and the American firm Walker and McGough.

Public misgivings Although brutalism was popular among architects and planners, it did not always meet with the approval of the public. There were several reasons for this. Block-like concrete façades that looked well in the light of India or the South of France did not suit northern light so well, and concrete that started out clean quickly began to look grey and grubby. In addition, in the post-war climate of rapid reconstruction, many brutalist buildings were poorly constructed.

Perhaps the greatest problem was with the use of brutalism in housing schemes. Inspired by Le Corbusier's *Unité d'Habitation*, many architects and planners laid out concrete housing schemes on a large scale. These schemes usually exploited fashionable planning theories that separated cars and pedestrians, providing access to flats via elevated walkways. They packed in hundreds, sometimes thousands of flats, often next to green spaces and incorporated the latest in modern technology.

But the pedestrian 'streets in the sky' became the haunts of muggers, poor maintenance turned the flats into dingy slums, the green spaces became windy wastelands and the modern conveniences broke down. Many such housing schemes became bywords for deprivation and brutalism seemed uncannily well named.

A source of controversy Critics of brutalism, such as the Prince of Wales, have attacked both the uncompromising design of the buildings and the depressing living environment these structures often provide. As a result many brutalist buildings have had a short life, but conservation groups have campaigned against the demolition of notable examples, such as Plymouth's Tricorn Centre and the outstanding St Peter's Seminary.

Brutalism or new brutalism?

These two terms are often used interchangeably for the concrete architecture of the 1960s and 1970s. But some architectural critics distinguish between the two, using 'brutalism', to mean the strictly zoned planning and high-rise blocks advocated by CIAM, and 'new brutalism' to describe the *béton brut* architecture described by Rayner Banham in his book *The New Brutalism* (1966), practised by the Smithsons and others, and exemplified by Plymouth's Tricorn Centre (right).

Meanwhile some brutalist buildings, especially university buildings from Yale to Chicago, have survived because they are well-designed structures fit for their purpose. The Johnson Art Museum at Cornell University, Ithaca, New York, designed in a dramatic brutalist style by I.M. Pei is a case in point. Such structures demonstrate that, in spite of the disasters, the better example of Brutalism will survive.

the condensed idea
Concrete without compromise

39 Neorationalism

The Italian movement known there as *la Tendenza* explored a way of building that was at once new and responsive to the shapes, forms and city plans of the past. Offering a voice of reason in opposition to the loud cries of modernism and postmodernism, it has become known outside Italy as neorationalism.

Many of the great architectural ideas of the late 20th century represent architects finding ways of moving beyond the modernism that had dominated architecture from the 1920s to the 1960s. Postmodernism, with its playfulness, its glorification of the commercial culture of Las Vegas, its off-hand historical references, was one route. But for some it was too brash, too consumerist. And brash consumerism, whether in the form of poorly detailed skyscrapers, glitzy cinemas or plastic shop fronts, was certainly taking over many a town centre.

The city and memory Against this background a number of architects, especially in Italy, began to look differently at cities and urban forms. Rather than aspiring to create brand-new ideal cities from scratch, as the modernists had done, architects and planners looked at old cities as places of interest from which they could learn. Cities are repositories of memory and hold important lessons about how society has evolved. Studying a city – how its buildings, plots, blocks, streets, squares and overall plan have changed through time – can tell us much about the past and help illuminate the present.

timeline

1966
Aldo Rossi publishes *The Architecture of the City*

1970–73
Rossi's Gallaretese housing scheme, Milan, under construction

Italian architects, theorists and historians responded well to these types of ideas about the history and form of the city. Their work bore fruit in a range of activities, from building-restoration projects to books, such as urban historian Leonardo Benevolo's huge and stimulating *The History of the City*. Aldo Rossi, the founder of the neorationalist movement, was also a writer, and his 1966 book, *The Architecture of the City*, also addressed these issues.

New and old The neorationalists worked against this background of historical awareness, of studying the shape or morphology of the city and of responding to current needs in the light of past heritage. So they were keen to build sensitively, but imaginatively in the great cities of Europe – and to avoid their domination by modernism, by the brash values of consumerist society or by the often crass designs of the communist countries of eastern Europe. They wanted to build new buildings, but structures that showed an awareness of and sensitivity to the past.

The movement emerged most strongly in Italy, where architects had the opportunity to learn from stunning historical cities. Rossi was also stimulated by the paintings of Giorgio de Chirico, haunting, surreal canvases in which strong, raking light plays on the details of quiet city squares and streets, picking out arcades, towers, monuments and statues. Rossi's work, exemplified by his cemetery buildings in Modena, evokes a similar atmosphere, with arch-lined 'streets', a pale red-walled ossuary with a pattern of square openings in the wall and quiet, open spaces.

> **The Tendenza was clearly an attempt to save both architecture and the city from being overrun by the all-pervasive forces of megalopolitan consumerism.**
>
> Kenneth Frampton, *Modern Architecture: A Critical History*

1972	**1980**	**1988–93**
Work begins on Mario Botta's school at Morbio Inferiore, Switzerland	Work begins on Rossi's cemetery buildings at Modena	Galician Centre for Contemporary Art, Santiago de Compostela, Spain

From building to product

The classical geometry of neorationalist buildings can be applied to much smaller forms than those of buildings, and some architects of the movement have also worked in product design. Aldo Rossi, for example, produced several designs for Alessi, including a striking stockpot called La Cupola (below right). It is based on a simple, shiny, metal cylinder topped by a hemispherical, dome-like lid. Mario Botta's pitcher (below left), also designed for Alessi, is likewise based on a cylinder, but with its top sliced off at a steep angle, rather like the roof of one of his buildings.

There is something in the pure forms and monumental quality of these buildings that recalls the vast unbuilt projects of those great French masters of the 18th-century age of reason, Boullée and Ledoux (see page 57). The French architects' big abstract forms – Boullée's plan to build a spherical monument to Isaac Newton 152 metres (500 ft) in diameter, for example – have a similar quality and this is revealed in the respective architects' drawings. Rossi's aerial perspective of the cemetery project shows the buildings casting long, dark shadows that recall Boullée's work.

Neorationalism began in Italy, spearheaded by Rossi's writings and by a book by another Italian architect, Giorgio Grassi, *La costruzione logica dell'architettura*. It bore fruit in works such as Rossi's housing scheme in the Gallaratese district of Milan and his reconstruction of the damaged Teatro Carlo Felice in Genoa.

Beyond Italy But many buildings influenced by the movement have been created outside Italy, making similar play with archetypal shapes and strange, tantalizing openings, as if conjuring up the ghosts of past buildings, but also suggesting that there is something interesting and different inside.

Some of the buildings of the Portuguese architect Álvaro Siza work in this way – his Galician Centre for Contemporary Art at Santiago de Compostela, for example, a huge, apparently simple form with dramatic horizontal 'slices' cut out of it that seem to invite the visitor inside.

One of the most successful architects influenced by these ideas is Mario Botta, the Swiss designer of a wide range of buildings characterized by strong and evocative forms. In France H.E. Ciriani showed the influence of neorationalism in a housing complex at Marne-la-Valée near Paris. And in Germany Mathias Ungers and J.P. Kleihues have worked in a similar way to the Italian neorationalists, setting sensitive new buildings in historic town centres.

Many cities in western Europe have benefited from these architects' sensitive approach to urban design and form, reminding us that new buildings can sit comfortably beside old ones, while adding something fresh to the ever-changing urban mix.

the condensed idea
Sensitivity in urban form

40 Archigram

The British group Archigram formed in the 1960s as a forum for architectural discussions and ideas. Its projects existed mainly on paper, but its ideas were highly influential. The members of Archigram preferred popular culture to the heroic high-culture of modernism, and proposed an architecture in which there were no buildings in the conventional sense – instead there were plug-in modules and adaptable, disposable structures in bright, Pop-Art colours.

The avant-garde architectural group Archigram flourished in London during the 1960s. Archigram was a rich mixture of people – of the main six, three (Warren Chalk, Dennis Crompton and Ron Herron) were experienced architects whose designs had been built, and three (Peter Cook, David Greene, and Mike Webb) were young, inexperienced and full of not always practical ideas. This combination of experienced practitioners and bright young ideas men produced a unique mix, able to think in new ways and propose radical design directions.

Tech and pop The architecture of Archigram took its inspiration from the latest technology: spacecraft, oil rigs and underwater structures. They were also influenced by contemporary culture: pop art, comics, the Beatles, throwaway packaging. Architecturally, they were interested in the lightweight structures of the American Buckminster Fuller (see page 140–3), as well as in the ideas of the futurists, who saw cities as machines.

timeline
1958
Mike Webb designs a project for the Furniture Manufacturers' Association, in the bowellist style

Bowellism

In 1958 the architect Mike Webb, soon to be a member of Archigram, designed a project for a headquarters building for the Furniture Manufacturers' Association. The proposed building, which looked like a collection of gigantic tubes, cylinders and containers, was all curved corners and rounded walls. It was the most famous design of a lost architectural movement, which, because its buildings resembled human intestines, became known as bowellism. These curvaceous forms, although unbuilt, were influential in 1960s' design and in the way in which high-tech buildings sometimes displayed the 'guts' of their structure on the outside.

This extraordinary mix of characters and influences led to an architecture in which the conventional distinctions could be broken down. Archigram conceived megastructures, but not in the form of skyscrapers or the 'heroic' structures of modernism. Among their most famous ideas was the Walking City – a structure that looked like a giant insect on metal legs. Turning inhabitants into nomads, these walking communities could stop at service stations where they could stock up with supplies. They were also designed to provide a protected habitat in the event of a nuclear war.

Another Archigram project, the Instant City, was more a happening than a structure. It would arrive – drawings show it carried by hot-air balloons – in a drab town and stimulate it with the addition of performances, structures and new technologies. This instant stimulation, it was argued, would awaken potential intelligence and creativity in the community, and local people would then be hooked up to new networks, leaving a grid of connected communities in place after the travelling circus of the Instant City had moved on.

1963

The Living Cities exhibition at the ICA, London, brings Archigram to wide public notice

1964

Ron Herron develops his 'Walking Cities' project and Peter Cook conceives the Plug-In City

1969

The Instant City is proposed as a way of revitalizing run-down urban centres

The modular city Plug-In City proposed a vast framework into which could be fitted countless standard 'modules'. Put simply, this sounds like an extension of existing ideas about prefabrication. But Archigram took the notion much further, and much deeper. One way in which they proposed to do this was in the field of transport. They were dissatisfied with trains and petrol-driven cars, which they saw as smelly, dangerous and demanding of space in the form of tracks and roads. They saw an alternative in the forms of the electric car, which was clean and compact. They tried to treat it as a mobile piece of furniture, integrating it with buildings in a way that was impossible with conventional vehicles.

Archigram turned many accepted notions upside down. Houses were replaced with living pods with curved, organic forms, or with portable dwellings, or with suits that contained a life-support system. Buildings moved, or grew, or were turned inside-out. It seemed to be a world of infinite possibilities and of optimism about the possibilities offered by technology.

A means of communication The group's ideas were highly influential, in part because the members of Archigram were good publicists and teachers. They published their ideas in a broadsheet (itself called *Archigram*), which sold all over the world. Illustrated with bold, comic-like drawings, these publications were a breath of fresh air.

The group also found vocal supporters in critics such as Rayner Banham who publicized their ideas still more widely. The architect Hans Hollein, who contributed to some of the Archigram publications, saw the power of all this writing and drawing when he described their architecture as 'a means of communication'.

❛To see architecture as much the natural outcome of circumstance as any other product or situation is an extremely healthy attitude.❜

Peter Cook, *Experimental Architecture*

Skins

Many Archigram structures took a kind of organic form. 'Living pods' had curved sides and ceilings; Walking Cities resembled insects; cylinders and other rounded forms abounded in their work. Many of these structures were covered with 'skins' of various types, evoking the use of new materials in architecture – canvas, plastic or glass fibre. These were lightweight coverings, a far cry from the heavy and solid materials, from concrete to timber, used in most buildings. But some architects and engineers took them up and made innovative structures with them. Frei Otto's stunning tent-like structures for the 1972 Munich Olympics (above) are famous examples.

A lasting influence All the writings and drawings brought Archigram great respect among other architects. Although their drawings and Pop-Art-inspired ideas have a strong period flavour, their ability to think in different ways contains lessons that go far beyond the 1960s. They had a powerful influence on the hi-tech movement. Their creative way with frameworks and 'floating' service structures left its vivid mark on buildings such as the Pompidou Centre in Paris. And their ideas continue to be examined by architects into the 21st century who want to look at their practice in new ways.

the condensed idea
Tech meets pop

41 Metabolist architecture

The Japanese group known as the Metabolists proposed a new kind of architecture based on values of adaptability and change. Their visionary designs included cities floating in the ocean and modular towers structured like enormous spirals or branching trees. Few of their projects were built but they made architects and designers think in new ways that were responsive to the pace of change in 20th-century society.

In the 1960s Japan's economy was growing rapidly after the recovery from the Second World War. Technological developments were moving quickly. The population was growing, too. Where did Japan's architects stand in this period of rapid change? To a group of them, it seemed that the times demanded a different type of architecture.

Adaptable architecture Buildings needed to be adaptable and flexible, but modern architecture, with its love of heavy materials such as concrete and tall structures like the skyscraper, seemed intent on producing buildings that could not adapt at all. So the new architecture should be based not on permanence or the premises of modernism, but on technology and adaptability. The Japanese group founded a new movement to embrace these ideas, and called themselves the Metabolists.

The Metabolists – rather like the British group Archigram (see page 160–163) – were looking for ways of designing flexible structures that

timeline

1958	1960
Kiyonori Kikutake designs Sky House, Tokyo	World Design Conference, Tokyo; Metabolist manifesto published

could grow organically. They were ambitious enough to want these structures to be on a huge scale, but, because Japan was a crowded island with a growing population, wanted to make the best use of the available land.

A culture of change It was not just the response to overcrowding that made the Metabolists a group with a grounding in Japanese culture and needs. They were also responding to a deep sense in Japan of the impermanence of their built environment. Japan's cities have been regularly destroyed – in earthquakes, floods, volcanic eruptions and in war – both in the conflicts of the 15th and 16th centuries and in the Second World War. Because so many of Japan's buildings were made of wood, they were virtually obliterated in each of these disasters, and had to be built again from scratch. The Metabolists' growing, adapting architecture seemed an appropriate response to this history of continuous change.

The group launched their movement at the World Design Conference in 1960, which took place in Tokyo, and produced a manifesto called *Metabolism: Proposals for a New Urbanism*. This document publicized a number of the architects' proposals, notably several designed by a leader of the movement, Kiyonori Kikutake. Kikutake had already caught the eye of Japanese architects with his Sky House of the late 1950s. This consisted of a single block raised on piers; when more space was required, additional rooms could be suspended below this main structure.

> **Unlike the architecture of the past, contemporary architecture must be . . . capable of meeting the changing requirements of the contemporary age.**
>
> Kiyonori Kikutake, *quoted in J. Donat's World Architecture*

1970
Metabolist designs shown at the Osaka Exposition

1972
Nagakin Capsule Tower, designed by Kisho Kurokawa, completed

Growing cities and skyscrapers Kikutake's other designs were still more radical. One was Marine City, in which prefabricated living 'pods' were attached to large cylinders floating in the ocean. The proposal was to arrange the cylinders in vast circles, and the resulting project had a beauty of form to match the daring of the concept. Another idea, developed by Noriaki Kurokawa, was to build – on dry land this time – helicoidal skyscrapers on to which living pods could be clipped.

Both of these projects combine the qualities at the heart of the Metabolist movement – they involve new technologies, they are large and ambitious, they have the scope for organic growth and they address the issue of Japan's crowded islands.

capsule hotels

The Capsule Tower remains unique, but it has influenced another peculiarly Japanese idea – the capsule hotel. The first example (Osaka's Capsule Inn) was designed by Kurokawa in the late 1970s and again embraces the key ideas of prefabrication, technology and space-saving. It and its many successors provide simple sleeping pods, just big enough for a bed; most also have televisions and wireless internet connections. There are usually communal bathrooms, restaurants and luggage-storage facilities. These minimal hotels have only caught on in Japan, where they are used mainly by businessmen.

The capsule concept Probably the most famous completed example of Metabolist architecture is the Nagakin Capsule Tower, Tokyo, designed by Kurokawa. This consists of two linked towers, from which some 140 small capsules – each of which is a miniature dwelling or office – are hung.

Each capsule is just 2.3 × 3.8 metres (8 × 12 ft) and contains a wall with built-in appliances (from refrigerator to television), a bed and a tiny bathroom. The capsules, which are basically steel boxes, were made and fitted out off-site and then bolted in place. In theory each capsule can be unbolted and replaced with a newer, upgraded one, although this has never actually happened.

The minimal accommodation in the Capsule Tower is another response to modern life on the part of the Metabolists. They observed that in the late 20th century, more and more once-private aspects of life – from meeting friends at cafés to listening to music – now take place in public. According to this logic, we need much less space at home than we used to. An apartment becomes a place in which to relax alone, watch television and sleep.

The Capsule Tower was an unusual Metabolist structure in that it was actually built. Most of the Metabolist projects, like those of their British counterparts Archigram, remain only as plans. Their ambitious names – Tower City, Wall City, Agricultural City – remain to tantalize architects. By the early 1970s the individual Metabolist architects had mostly moved on to more conventional and realistic practices. One of them, Kenzo Tange, became probably the most celebrated Japanese architect of the period, building more conventional buildings, but still using technology in striking and innovative ways.

the condensed idea
Easily adaptable architecture

42 Townscape

The townscape movement emerged after the Second World War as a way of looking at how towns grew organically and how planners should respect the visual richness produced by this organic growth. Although primarily a British movement, it had a wide influence as an alternative to the modernist attitude to looking at towns and redeveloping them.

Like many generations before them the architects of the modern movement had clear ideas of their perfect city. For most it was a city built from scratch, full of modernist towers and planned in zones – an area for work, another for play, another for housing. For most, it was also an ideal in which traffic was separated from pedestrians, a place of urban freeways and soaring overpasses.

Reconstruction After the Second World War architects and planners had their chance to put these theories into practice. If not entire cities, large swathes of towns and big new estates began to rise up where wartime bombing had given builders carte blanche. For many this was a brave new world in which towns, most of which had grown haphazardly over the centuries, could be properly planned for the first time.

This outlook resulted in the transformation of many cities – the 1950s' redevelopment of central Boston with its urban freeways, for example, or, in Britain, the construction of vast housing estates around cities such as Birmingham, not to mention the logical, grid-based planning of new towns such as Milton Keynes.

timeline

1944

The *Architectural Review* publishes articles called 'Townscape Casebook' and 'The Art of Making Urban Landscapes', starting the British townscape movement

> **❝. . . if at the end of it all the city appears dull, uninteresting and soulless, then it is not fulfilling itself. It has failed. The fire has been laid but nobody has put a match to it.❞**
>
> Gordon Cullen, The Concise Townscape

Learning from the past But not everyone saw urban planning in this way. For some, the old haphazard way in which towns had grown, with their mixture of architectural styles and often narrow, winding streets, was a good thing. It was visually stimulating and indicative of a culturally rich past. Perhaps surprisingly, one place where this alternative view was voiced was Britain's *Architectural Review* – a leading journal that had often championed modernism. In 1944, with the prospect of the end of the war at last realistic, its editor, Ivor de Wolfe, called for a more diverse, pluralistic approach to town planning.

Ivor de Wolfe and his colleague Gordon Cullen saw that the general public would not take kindly to a 'new Jerusalem, all open space and white concrete'. Planners should instead study what was good about our existing towns and cities. They should remember that the ideals of the 19th-century picturesque movement (see pages 48–51), in which architects and gardeners placed buildings in landscapes with an eye on their artistic effect, could also be applied to urban settings. In other words, townscape was as important as landscape.

Explaining townscape In articles in the *Architectural Review* and in books such as *Townscape* and *The Concise Townscape*, Cullen outlined these ideas. He spent a lot of time and space analysing the buildings, streets, lanes and squares of towns, old and new, to demonstrate how they worked and what was good about them visually. With the aid of

1951	**1960**	**1961**
Gordon Cullen is part of the team working at the Festival of Britain, in which ideas of variety and picturesque incident are at the heart of the design	Cullen begins work as a planning advisor in New Delhi	Cullen publishes his book *Townscape*, later reissued in a shortened edition as *The Concise Townscape*

photographs and his own clear and evocative drawings, he showed how our experiences of urban spaces change as we move through them.

Urban features

Townscape identifies many features like those in the view of Oxford (below) that make city scenery distinctive. Here are a few of the most important.

- **Focal point** Structures that form a focus – towers, statues, columns, crosses.
- **Enclosure** Quiet, human-scale precincts, such as squares or courtyards.
- **Viscosity** The way in which people 'slow down' – to talk, meet, window-shop, buy a newspaper – in a healthy urban environment.
- **Vista** The way in which the eye can be led through a scene – vistas may be open, grandiose or screened, for example, by trees.
- **Punctuation and incident** Buildings and objects that catch the eye and give structure to a townscape.
- **Scale** Our perception of the size and prominence of buildings and other structures.

Cullen was especially revealing about the variety of townscape – how different sizes of building, projecting and recessing façades, visual 'incident' and 'punctuation', changing street widths, bends, curves and mysterious openings all enhance our experience of a town. And these features, of course, were quite the opposite of the uniformity proposed by most modernist planners.

Organic growth The rich variety of cities that had grown organically, with their seemingly random mix of large and small, old and new buildings, entranced Cullen. And he was convinced that when others understood it, they would be entranced, too – the traditional organic city was for him an immense source of sheer visual pleasure. The opposite of this was what Cullen called 'Prairie planning': the same house design repeated endlessly against a background of uniformly wide streets, dull street furniture and featureless, unfenced gardens.

During the 1960s there was a running argument between the advocates of modernist planning and the followers of de Wolfe and Cullen, with their more pluralist approach. The modernists criticized Cullen for his emphasis on old cities. The townscape lobby attacked the modernists for the tedium and inhumanity of their plans.

Neither camp was wholly victorious. Many cities were redeveloped along modernist lines, but Cullen's arguments were used by those favouring more sensitive and tactful development. But Cullen's influence went further than this. He taught several generations how to look at towns more inquisitively and critically, and how to appreciate the way in which towns develop organically, and his work was followed up by later writers and journalists. Directly or indirectly, most of us are probably more aware of our urban surroundings because of the work of Gordon Cullen.

the condensed idea
Richness and complexity in urban form

43 Structuralism

In the 1950s a group of architects broke away from the mainstream modernist organization CIAM and began to take architecture in new directions. These structuralist architects turned to traditional architecture, social structures and the power of place for their inspiration, and produced buildings that at once looked modern and were designed in a more user-aware way than those of the high modernists of the previous generation.

Structuralism was a term used widely across many different disciplines, from anthropology to literary criticism, at various times during the second half of the 20th century. In architecture the word is used specifically for a movement that emerged in Holland in the late 1950s and bore fruit in the work of architects such as Jacob Bakema and Aldo van Eyck in Europe, Kenzo Tange in Japan and Louis Kahn in the USA.

Team 10 Bakema and van Eyck were members of Team 10 (also known as Team X). They were a group of architects who broke away from CIAM, the congress of architects who, enthused with the modernist ideas of Le Corbusier, had been so influential in European architecture. Team 10 was not an architectural practice, but a group of architects who met to discuss, teach and publish their ideas. They included the founders of British new brutalism (see pages 152–155) as well as the Dutch structuralists.

timeline

1957–60
Municipal Orphanage, Amsterdam, by Aldo van Eyck, built

1959–65
Salk Institute, La Jolla, California, by Louis Kahn

'Architecture is the three-dimensional expression of human behaviour.'

Jacob Bakema

The structuralists wanted to create buildings that reflected the social structures of the people who were to use them. They therefore looked for the archetypal behaviour patterns that people exhibit, and searched for mirrors of these in traditional or vernacular architecture. But they also saw that architecture, for all it might look for inspiration to these eternal patterns, must also be adaptable and flexible, responsive to growth and change. Architecture should be responsive to place, too.

The idea of the importance of the profound structures of society comes from anthropology, in particular the work of Claude Levi-Strauss, whose work had inspired structuralist anthropologists and experts in linguistics.

Place and symbol The search for archetypal qualities that also respond to the specifics of place led Aldo van Eyck to study traditional architecture in Africa – especially the buildings of the Dogon people of Mali. Here he found a powerful sense of symbolism – in the way the Dogon planned their buildings with each space allocated its own status, and with strong meaning attached to features such as gates and doorways.

So structuralist architecture was inspired by traditional forms and symbols – it was in part a rejection of the modernist, technocratic architecture of Le Corbusier and his followers in CIAM. But van Eyck and his colleagues did not build mud huts; they sought a way of using the symbolic forms of traditional architecture in structures made of modern materials for modern people.

1966–70	1969–75	1970–72
Montessori School, Delft, by Herman Hertzberger, constructed	Byker Wall housing development, Newcastle upon Tyne, designed by Ralph Erskine	Centraal Beheer Insurance office, Apeldoorn, under construction

Housing These ideas lie behind many buildings and urban plans that the structuralists produced from the 1960s to the 1980s. In housing, for example, there were two strong tendencies, one involving a return to more flexible spaces rather than houses rigidly divided into rooms with specific functions. This was seen as a modern response to the single-room dwellings common in pre-industrial societies. The other major

community architecture

During the 1970s a number of architects, working mainly on housing schemes in Britain, attempted to bring residents – the future users of the buildings – to the very heart of the design process. One of the most successful schemes was Byker Wall, Newcastle upon Tyne (right), where the architect, Team 10 member Ralph Erskine, moved his office to the site in order to keep the interaction between designers and users constant. Later architects took the process still further, helping occupants to build their own homes so that they truly 'owned' the entire process of design and construction. This true community architecture, practised by Charles Knevitt and Nick Wates, exploited low-tech building systems so that non-specialists could build with minimal training. It has helped to regenerate poor and run-down areas in several cities.

trend in housing was to do with public participation in planning and design. This was exemplified by the work of a number of British architects, including Ralph Erskine.

City and office Preoccupation with place also brought the structuralists into the realm of urban planning. They tried to revive the city street as a meaningful social experience. They tried to bring some of this skill in place-making to their office projects, too. Here it was a question of relating the small rooms and spaces that typify large office developments.

Herman Hertzberger succeeded in this in his Centraal Beheer Insurance building, Apeldoorn, in which small office units relate to one another across a central atrium, and where there is a good balance between private and communal spaces. Hertzberger saw this kind of building as a 'city within the city', and also related it to the casbahs and bazaars of Turkey and the Middle East.

Modern monumentality In America the work of Louis Kahn took structuralist ideas in new directions. Buildings such as his Salk Institute, La Jolla, California, beautifully express the way the structure is used, with laboratories and towers containing scientists' studies clearly expressed. But Kahn also brings a sense of monumentality to the complex, his two blocks of laboratories forming a powerful presence on the Institute's ocean-side site. An admirer of Greek temples and Roman basilicas, Kahn saw that we need big buildings that sit happily in their settings. This perception was another way in which the architects of structuralism and Team 10 found nurture from the roots of tradition.

the condensed idea
Built structures should mirror social structures

44 Regionalism

A number of architects have felt the need to counter the 'international' aspect of modern architecture. They prefer their buildings to express or respect the place where they are sited, and to draw for their inspiration on local culture. Known widely as regionalism, this attitude has added a richness and variety to the architecture of the late 20th century, and continues to influence architectural thinking.

In writing about the great modern buildings, most critics of the 20th century saw modern architecture as an international phenomenon. Encouraged by the title of the famous New York exhibition The International Style, the buildings of 20th-century 'masters', such as Le Corbusier and Mies van der Rohe, were treated as a new beginning, as solutions to specific problems rather than responses to local conditions or regional styles. Their favourite materials – concrete, steel and glass – were the same the world over. Modern architecture, in this view, was international, but led by great pioneers from the Western world.

Place and modern architecture And yet these great pioneers did draw inspiration from specific places. Frank Lloyd Wright's Prairie Houses, for example, were conceived (and named) as a specifically American kind of dwelling, appropriate to the wide-open spaces of the Midwest. Le Corbusier was inspired by the traditional white houses of Greece. All modern architects worth the name absorbed and transformed influences from specific localities, adapting these influences in the process but leaving some trace of them in their buildings, too.

timeline

1960
Brasilia officially inaugurated
as Brazil's new capital

1964
Tokyo Olympics feature
the gymnasium designed
by Kenzo Tange

A later generation of architects saw this clearly. Many of these people came from parts of the world outside the 'western' orbit of the early modernists. They wanted to design in a modern way, but to acknowledge the traditions and geographies of their particular parts of the globe and to create buildings that were at one with their setting. Not for them the idea of putting down a modernist steel-and-glass box anywhere, irrespective of climate or local environment. Architectural writers have coined the term 'regionalism' for their distinctive and diverse brands of modern architecture.

World-wide responses One place where this can be seen clearly is in the major public buildings of Brasilia, the purpose-built capital city of Brazil. Brasilia's core was built in the late 1950s under principal planner Lúcio Costa and architect Oscar Niemeyer. Its architecture needed to be at once modern, but also expressive of Brazil's identity and culture. While designing in a recognizably modernist idiom, Niemeyer introduced the curves of the Brazilian landscape into his buildings. The Chamber of Deputies, shaped like a concrete bowl, the Senate with its white dome and the cathedral with its curving concrete ribs all contribute to this effect.

Other architects engaged on smaller projects also drew richly on regional cultures. The Japanese Kenzo Tange brought together traditional Japanese architecture and modernism. The Mexican Luis Barragán brought to modernism a feeling for colour, light and sensuousness that drew heavily on the art and tradition of Mexico. Geoffrey Bawa, from Sri Lanka, developed what has been termed a 'tropical modernism' in response to conditions in southern Asia. Hassan Fathy worked with appropriate technologies, such as mud-brick, in his native Egypt.

1966

Luis Barragán designs the Folke Egerstrom house and stables, San Cristóbal

1984

University of Ruhuna, Matara, Sri Lanka, moves to new buildings designed by Geoffrey Bawa

Regionalism and vernacular

Sometimes planners and architects respond to local building traditions by adopting the vernacular style of the area. This can work, especially when those involved are absorbed in the local way of building and are creating a traditional building type – a house, for example, or a farm building – using local materials. It can also succeed when an architect responds to local traditions, as in Barragán's work (below). But the mindless imitation of vaguely vernacular styles to disguise buildings such as supermarkets or offices is rarely successful. The form of the building is already decided and designed inside and the vernacular shell acts merely as an inoffensive coating.

Regionalism shines through the work of the likes of Barragán and Tange, but pervades the work of other, less well known architects, too. Even in the West, where commercialism and fashion too often blunt the cutting edge of architecture, practitioners such as Andrew Batey and Mark Mack, working in Napa Valley, California, produce site-sensitive houses of great quality.

> **Architecture is a violation of landscape; it cannot simply be integrated, it must create a new equilibrium.**
>
> Mario Botta

These architects and others whose work is inspired by place and locality are a diverse group. They do not constitute an architectural 'school'. Barragán, for example, has been called a minimalist (though this belies the richness of his forms and colours), while Fathy's work is closer to the vernacular architecture of his homeland. But the work of all of them points to something crucial to architecture: that the role of place is central.

Indigenous wisdom It is no accident that many of these architects work in the developing world, where resources are often scarce, technologies sometimes restricted, but local traditions rich and giving. Even in a developed country such as Australia, architects have found much to learn from the landscape and the wisdom of its indigenous inhabitants. Glenn Murcutt, an architect admired for houses that respond well to Australia's landscape, traditions and climate, has found a way of summing up this position in an Aboriginal proverb. 'Touch this earth lightly' is his motto, and his houses, light, open to the breeze, raised above the ground on slender posts, embody these words to perfection.

In the 21st century this message is as important as it has ever been. Every step we take we are encouraged to respect the environment or protect the planet. Buildings make a profound impact on locality, resources and lives, so in architecture above all else it is essential to respect place, as the practitioners of green architecture (see pages 200–203) know. The power of place is still strong.

the condensed idea
Respect the power of place

45 Postmodernism

Postmodernism is the term used to describe the brash, diverse, witty and colourful architecture that emerged in the late 1960s as a reaction to the simple, restrained architecture of the modern movement. The postmodernists saw their new way of thinking about buildings as stimulating and liberating, and their irreverent approach has had a lasting influence, even on architects who followed other paths.

In the years after the Second World War modernism dominated the world of architecture. Architects valued modernism because it gave them a rigorous way of thinking about architecture – assess the function of your building, design it logically and its form will emerge naturally. Glass-and-steel towers, concrete apartment blocks and similar buildings were the result of this functionalist approach.

Restoring the missing ingredients But some architects were unhappy with the way modernism cut itself off from many traditional aspects of their art. The modernists looked down on ornament, cut themselves off from the past and produced serious buildings that lacked any dimension of wit or humour. What would happen if these ingredients were put back into architecture? One answer was provided by the architects who rebelled against functionalism to create the architectural style that was later dubbed postmodernism.

The movement began in North America and at its forefront was the architect Robert Venturi, whose book *Complexity and Contradiction in Architecture* appeared in 1966. In it, he argued for a more ambiguous,

timeline

1963
Robert Venturi designs the Vanna Venturi house, Chestnut Hill, Philadelphia, for his mother

1966
Robert Venturi publishes *Complexity and Contradiction in Architecture*

paradoxical approach as opposed to the simplicity of modernist architecture. It was a theme he pursued in another book, *Learning from Las Vegas*, which he co-wrote with his fellow architects Denise Scott-Brown (who was also his wife) and Steven Izenour. The authors praised the eclectic, commercial and brash in American architecture.

Allusion

When he designed a house for his mother (below), Robert Venturi said that the front was meant to evoke a picture of a house, especially one from the 18th century. The arch above the doorway is one 18th-century allusion; the way that the gable suggests a triangular classical pediment is another; the horizontal moulding, like a string course on an older building, is a third. But all of these features are only hinted at: the 'pediment' is split at the apex by a large opening; the 'arch' is interrupted by the gap and the lintel over the doorway. Even this is not the whole story – the house also contains allusions (such as the strip windows) to buildings by modernist guru Le Corbusier. The postmodernists liked to have things both ways.

1978
Charles Moore designs the Piazza, d'Italia, New Orleans, which he fills with brightly coloured, mock-classical elements

1979–84
Philip Johnson AT&T Building (now Sony Plaza Building) is constructed in New York

1980
Michael Graves designs the Portland Public Services Building, Portland, Oregon

Humour and architecture At the same time Venturi designed a series of buildings that embodied architectural jokes. The house he designed for his mother, for example, at Chestnut Hill, Philadelphia, hinted at classical forms, but in a refined kind of way that only architects understood.

Soon, others were picking up the idea and running with it, producing buildings that contained much more obvious jokes and references to the past. One of the most famous was the AT&T Building in New York, which takes the form of a classical skyscraper with a top like an 18th-century Chippendale chair. This postmodern monument of 1979–84 was designed by Philip Johnson, who had previously worked with Mies van der Rohe and been a champion of modernism.

Ornament and allusion The 1970s and 1980s saw a variety of architects adopting this more diverse, amusing, style in which it was no longer considered incorrect to add ornament to buildings or to make allusions to the architecture of the past. As well as Venturi, American architects Michael Graves and Charles Moore took up the cause with colourful, allusive buildings. Others followed overseas, from Ricardo Bofill in Spain to Kenzo Tange in Japan. Meanwhile the British-resident, American architect and writer Charles Jencks had coined the term postmodernism for what all these architects were doing.

High art and low art

For much of history architects tried to emphasize the high seriousness of their work. Providing buildings that are both attractive and functional is an important, costly business and deserves to be taken seriously, after all. The postmodernists tried to look at their profession in the opposite way. They sought out what it could have in common with 'low' or popular culture: colourful advertising signs, pop art, the brash diversity of the American main street. By combining these elements with classical ones they were creating a new mix of visual stimuli.

> **❝Where the Modern masters' strength lay in constancy, ours should lie in diversity.❞**
>
> Robert Venturi, *A View from the Campidoglio*

Irony and paradox These architects looked to the past for inspiration, but did so with a paradoxical or ironic twist. They would hold up a building on classical columns, but the columns would be covered in a modern material such as steel or painted some bright unclassical colour. They would add finials to the top of a building, but shape these finials in some modern form so that they looked like egg-cups or space rockets. They would use classical features but arrange them asymmetrically, so that they looked new and odd.

The name postmodernism (sometimes abbreviated PoMo) stuck and it was applied to all types of buildings that included an element of parody and pastiche, or made amusing patterns with windows, or opposed bright and brash colours to the shades of white and grey favoured by the modernists. Architecture was catching up with the visual arts, which had been celebrating the joys of pop art and popular culture for years, and was enjoying itself greatly in the process.

Postmodernism showed architects that they could be eclectic, and that they could respond to the human need for stimulation and surprise that was not always fulfilled by modernism. In doing this they not only produced interesting buildings, but they also opened the way for other more radical ways of designing buildings eclectically and surprisingly, widening our horizons in the process.

the condensed idea
Pop and history can mix

46 Contemporary classicism

Frustrated by the limitations of most contemporary architecture, a few architects have returned to classicism. Although they have suffered criticism and charges of pastiche from the architectural establishment, their buildings are often well received by the public. They have shown, in housing especially but in other building types, too, that classicism still offers a rich and adaptable architectural vocabulary.

The past few decades have seen an increasing discontent with modern architecture – with 'concrete-and-glass' modernism in the tradition of Le Corbusier especially, but with all forms of building that use 'modern' materials in 20th-century ways. Objectors point to the failures of 1960s' and 1970s' brutalist housing schemes, to the high heating and air conditioning costs incurred by users of buildings with glass curtain walls, to the short life of many concrete buildings. Above all, they are disappointed by the impoverished visual language of modernism. For some, the answer is to return to the classical tradition.

For many architects this was anathema. The central method of modernism – examine users' needs, concentrate on function and let the building's form follow that function – was central to their practice and beliefs. To turn back the clock to the 18th century, or to the Renaissance or even to the Romans, seemed to them retrogressive and irrelevant.

timeline

1936
Raymond Erith is commissioned to design the Great House, Dedham, Essex, beginning his career as a classicist

1961
Library, Lady Margaret Hall, Oxford, by Raymond Erith, is completed

Morality and Architecture

In his influential book *Morality and Architecture*, British architectural historian David Watkin argued that modernist architecture has been discussed in terms of the philosophical idea of the *Zeitgeist*, or spirit of the age. Modernist architecture, it had been argued, was good and rational because it was adapted to the *Zeitgeist* and was based on society's needs. Classical architecture, however, was condemned by the modernists because it grew from a past age, and therefore it was irrelevant or immoral today to design in such a style. Watkin and the defenders of classicism, though, point to the fact that the classical style embodies civilized values and provides a vocabulary of architecture than can be endlessly adapted.

Objections to classicism On the one hand, one set of objections comes from those who believe that classicism is simply a set of ornaments that are stuck on to a building in a pastiche of Georgian or Renaissance architecture. Proponents of classicism, such as contemporary British architects Quinlan Terry and Robert Adam, on the other hand, claim that classicism is actually highly functional. Classical house plans work and can be adapted to suit modern requirements; classical details, such as mouldings and orders (see pages 4–7), can be used to guide people through a building – to signpost the difference between a living room door and a cupboard door, or to point up a building's main entrance.

Objectors also point out that the classicism of past ages was used for a relatively narrow range of buildings – such as houses, churches and town halls. Can classical architecture really be adapted for airports, factories and other contemporary types of buildings? Classicists answer that their way of working is highly adaptable. The classical architects of the Renaissance were very inventive, and today's architects should be inventive, too.

1984–87
Richmond Riverside development, by Quinlan Terry, is built in a mixture of classical styles from the 17th to 19th centuries

1993
Construction begins at Poundbury, the development sponsored by the Prince of Wales and designed in a mixture of classical and traditional styles

classicism and light

One of the beauties of classical architecture is the way in which its forms – mouldings, rustication, columns – catch the light and shade, giving interest and satisfaction to a façade or interior in a way that changes with the moving sun. This was vital in times when there was little or no artificial light, but still gives buildings richness today. Quinlan Terry has pointed out, for example, how the combination of circles and squares at the top of a Tuscan column creates a combination of hard and soft shadows.

Choice of materials Another question surrounds materials. Modernist architecture and the host of styles and outlooks of the past few decades – from postmodernism to deconstructivism – make use of all the materials today's technology can produce. Classicists tend to use traditional materials – stone, brick, tile, wood, lime mortar. They argue that not only do these materials work visually in classical buildings, but they are also longer lasting and cheaper to maintain than modern concrete. And when they age, they do so more gracefully.

And to the surprise of many, there are still craftworkers who not only can work these materials with skill, but do so with pleasure. Their work may cost more than that of conventional builders, but it lasts and works.

> **Although the spiritual, political, material and temporal influences are crystallized in wood and stone, and expressed in classical forms, the classical grammar remains neutral; like the paint on the artist's palette.**
>
> **Quinlan Terry,** in his essay 'Seven Misunderstandings About Classical Architecture'

These craftspeople have responded to the plans and instructions of architects, such as Raymond Erith, Terry and Adam, who have kept classicism alive.

The art of compromise? Predictably, many in the architectural establishment have been unimpressed. They point to such schemes as Terry's mixed-use development at Richmond Riverside, London, where elegant, classical façades hide modern, open-plan offices. This, opponents said, was architectural pastiche of the worst kind. Defenders pointed out that the design was a compromise, but one that worked in practical terms – passers-by could enjoy the façades, while office workers benefited from the usable spaces within.

And perhaps the verdict on contemporary classicism is a compromise, too. It works in a range of buildings in the hands of a master designer such as Raymond Erith. More widely, Classical houses are still satisfying and rewarding for many residents. Classicism can work well in sensitive historical environments, from Oxford, England, to Boston, Massachusetts.

The use of traditional materials, if they are sourced locally, also makes sense in terms of reducing transport costs and carbon emissions. Traditional buildings, too, are often cheaper to heat and cool than modernist or high-tech ones built with more lavish areas of glass. A world that can accept the bizarre angles and spaces of deconstructivism and the wayward ways of postmodernism must have a place for classicism, too.

the condensed idea
Classicism still works today

47 High-tech

Most people are familiar with the term 'high-tech', a combination of words that is used widely to describe the type of design that uses advanced technology and that puts this technology firmly on display. Since the 1970s there have also been 'high-tech' buildings – structures that wear their technology on their sleeves in a variety of ways, dramatically provoking the shock of the new.

High-tech (or, sometimes, hi-tech) architecture is closely associated with a number of architects who emerged, mostly in Britain, in the 1970s. These architects qualified at a time when the modernist ethos was still very strong and functionalism was seen as they key to good design.

Unorthodox influences This was the architectural orthodoxy of the time. But the young architects of the 1970s were also captivated by a number of unorthodox approaches – for example, the innovative 'Dymaxion' theories of Richard Buckminster Fuller (see pages 140–143), with his prefabricated metal houses and geodesic domes, and the revolutionary ideas of the Archigram group (see pages 160–163), with their plug-in modules and walking cities.

So prefabrication, the use of ready-made components, and the outward display of technology became key to these architects, who included Richard Rogers, Renzo Piano, Norman Foster, Nicholas Grimshaw and Michael Hopkins. The building that set the tone was the Pompidou Centre in Paris, designed by Richard Rogers and Renzo Piano, a building that famously displays all its services (escalators, ducts and

timeline
1971–7

Pompidou Centre, Paris, designed by Richard
Rogers and Renzo Piano, under construction

pipes) on the outside, leaving the interior for large, open-gallery spaces. The result is a colourful riot of a structure.

Signature buildings But subsequent high-tech buildings took a slightly different approach, especially in the work of Rogers and Norman Foster. Their signature buildings were Foster's Hong Kong and Shanghai Bank in Hong Kong and Rogers' London Lloyds Building. Both display structure and services such as elevators in an open, high-tech way. But they add something else – both buildings look as if they are made of beautifully machined, factory-made components, with everything immaculately finished. These structures look like finely honed machines.

The Lloyds Building has a gleaming metallic finish and services such as lifts are hung on the outside of the building. The Hong Kong and Shanghai Bank displays its structure to the world in the form of components such as vast trusses that were made in Britain and shipped out to Hong Kong. Features such as bathroom pods (recalling Buckminster Fuller's prefabricated Dymaxion bathrooms) were manufactured off-site and delivered complete and fully fitted out. All the finishes are smooth and machine-like.

The Hong Kong and Shanghai Bank looks so much like a machine made of bolted-together metal parts that there was even a rumour that the structure could be taken apart and moved if the bank fell foul of China's government when control of Hong Kong passed from Britain to China.

> **The artist no less than the scientist or the philosopher . . . works in a structured area of problems**
>
> Ernst Kris, *Psychoanalytic Explorations in Art*

1978–86	**1979–85**	**1992**
Lloyds Building, London, designed by Richard Rogers, under construction	Hong Kong and Shanghai Bank, designed by Norman Foster, under constructiony	Schlumberger Research Centre, Cambridge, designed by Michael Hopkins, built

High-tech as a style The beautifully finished appearance of the Lloyds Building and the Hong Kong and Shanghai Bank seemed to embody the old ideal of functionalism, with everything precisely engineered to provide users with the large, uncluttered office spaces and big central atria that they required. But actually the designs were more finely honed than they needed to be. The engineered machine aesthetic was in part an end in itself, a way of creating a high-tech image.

As a style, high-tech won Foster, Rogers and their colleagues many followers. The boom years of the 1980s saw many tall, shiny office towers that, in part at least, imitated their style without delivering such high quality. The term high-tech became popular as a way of describing everything from metal furniture to the design of science-fiction movies.

The atrium

Conventional skyscrapers consisted of largely similar, uniform-height floors of offices. Many clients in the late 20th century, however, wanted atria – big, high interior spaces. Atria act as meeting places, as access areas leading visitors to elevators and office floors and as awesome spaces to impress clients. The strong 'inside-out' structures in both the Lloyds and Hong Kong and Shanghai Bank buildings enabled their architects to create impressive multiple-height spaces in this way.

New directions Meanwhile, however, the most innovative high-tech architects had moved on. Nicholas Grimshaw and Michael Hopkins, for example, produced a wide range of innovative buildings, some of which took structures in new directions – for example, developing tent-like suspended structures that could cover a large area with lightweight materials.

Foster and others took technology in other directions, using computer design and modern materials to design buildings that were increasingly sensitive to environmental concerns. They showed that high-tech and green architecture could come together, and that an ecologically sound building did not have to be constructed of 'traditional' materials, such as wood and mud.

Tension structures

Tent-like structures, which were roofed with strong fabric suspended from cables attached to masts, were an innovative feature of high-tech architecture. Making use of modern fabrics coated with strengthening and weather-proofing materials, such as Teflon, they were sometimes justified because their lightness allowed buildings to be erected where the subsoil was too weak to support a conventional building. More often, however, the biggest benefit was in the dramatic appearance – the large, faceted shapes of Michael Hopkins's Schlumberger Research Centre, Cambridge, (below) is a good example.

For the next generation of architects, high-tech was an interesting episode that could be inspiring. It encouraged designers to think differently about materials, about ways of constructing buildings, and about prefabrication. Its influence lives on in the work of many – architects who do not want to imitate the 'machined' appearance of the Hong Kong and Shanghai Bank but who can respond with new experiments in design and structure.

the condensed idea
Polished technology on display

48 Alternative architecture

The search for sustainability takes people on long journeys. For some, the only way to live is to build outside the normal constraints of energy consumption, planning law and architectural convention. Some such people have created alternative communities of self-built, low-energy homes made from recycled materials. For its advocates this alternative architecture is the architecture of the future.

With its ideals of low energy consumption, green architecture is attractive to many, and some of the world's most prominent architectural practices are now designing energy efficiency into their buildings. But for some even this approach, which usually involves conventional structures, is not enough. They have sought to create an alternative architecture, using all types of recycled materials, from old car bodies and tyres to corrugated iron and earth to build cheap homes for themselves without the input of professional architects or builders.

Rethinking building Sometimes this approach produces the architecture of the shanty-town or plotland – resourceful, inventive and created on the fly. But some advocates of alternative architecture think through the design of buildings from first principles, producing a completely different type of building. The most outstanding examples of this are the structures called Earthships, pioneered in the 1970s by Michael Reynolds in the desert of New Mexico.

timeline

1972

Michael Reynolds builds his first house from recycled materials

Earthships usually have walls of earth-filled car tyres; they use these thick walls (sometimes with added earth insulation) to keep the warmth in during winter and the temperature down in summer. They use carefully positioned windows to maximize light and heat in the winter. They are usually off-the-grid buildings, contain equipment for collecting rainwater and recycling greywater, and feature solar panels and wind turbines to generate electricity.

On or off-grid

Off-grid buildings have to be highly thermally efficient, as well as having power-generation systems tuned to local conditions. Since in most places on the Earth the sun does not shine all day or the wind blow continuously, designers usually have to build in more than one way of producing power. In many places even these are not enough to produce all the power the occupants need – or, more commonly, may produce a surplus at some times of year and too little at others. As a result many green designs embody a compromise. They are connected to the grid, but supplement grid power with home-generated electricity, sometimes selling electricity back to the grid during periods of surplus.

Ways with walls Earth-and-tyre walls are strong and fire-resistant. Their large mass is designed to absorb heat from the sun during the day and they act as radiators, passing the heat to the interior when the outside temperature falls at night. Earth-and-tyre walls are also very cheap and easy to build by people with no particular building experience – provided they have plenty of time to perform the labour-intensive task of ramming the earth into the tyres. Originally conceived for the hot climate of New Mexico, the wall structure can be modified for other climates, and Earthships with concrete, sand-bag or adobe walls have been built in various locations. There are now Earthships in Europe and in most American states.

1990s
The Earthship concept comes under criticism after some owners complain of poor temperature control and leaky roofs

2000
Earthship Biotecture sets up a European office

2004
First British Earthship is completed, at Kinghorn Loch, Fife, Scotland

> **The experience of living in a ship ... requires dwellers to be autonomous from outside help.**
>
> Daniel Terdiman, from the article 'Life in an Earthship'

Some of these buildings are earth-sheltered – in other words, they are partially buried in the ground or shielded by banks of earth. Earth-sheltering maximizes the capacity of the building to store solar heat and pass it on slowly to the interior, making the house warmer in the winter and cooler during the summer. This way of enhancing heat efficiency is sometimes referred to as the 'thermal-flywheel effect'.

Other recycled materials used in Earthships include tin cans, which, joined together by concrete and plastered over, are often used for internal, non-load-bearing walls. Some buildings also have glass walls made from bottles, although the principal windows have panes of regular glass, facing towards the sun to maximize solar gain. Other window openings and skylights are carefully placed so that they provide natural ventilation, especially during hot periods, by bringing in cool air through a front window and pushing out rising warm air through a skylight.

New lifestyles Earthships have shown how groups of people can live without drawing on mains electricity. Until now, such houses have been built in relatively small numbers and are seen by many as experiments both in alternative architecture and in alternative living. The majority of examples are in places where the population density is very low. Building Earthships, and other houses with unconventional structures, is often much more challenging than tackling a regular building project because they do not conform to the standards local planners normally use to assess proposed buildings. However, as alternative architectural designs become more popular there are hopes that planners will become more open to unusual structures.

Moving towards the mainstream But as concerns about climate change grow and the recent instability in the economy continues to affect people across the globe, a solution that offers low-cost and low-energy housing could become more popular. And Earthship Biotecture, Michael Reynolds' firm that created the Earthship concept and has built many examples around the world, now claims that it can create buildings with a carbon footprint of zero – structures that heat and cool themselves without fuel and treat the waste products produced by the inhabitants. Alternative architecture could move nearer to the mainstream.

Tyre-wall construction

Earthship Biotecture recommend that two people work together when building tyre walls (below). One person shovels the earth into the tyre, while another stands by the tyre with a sledge hammer and rams in the earth as evenly as possible. When one tyre is full they move on to the next. Well-rammed walls like this are very strong, but may lack stiffness, so vertical strengthening ribs are sometimes inserted to give the wall extra rigidity.

the condensed idea
Recycle, renew, revitalize

49 Deconstructivism

Many buildings of the last two decades of the 20th century seemed to make their effect by means of fragmentation – they were structures that seemed about to topple over, or to break down conventional distinctions between up and down, left and right, inside and outside. These precarious-looking structures are often grouped together under the term deconstructivism. They are an endless source of visual, spatial and architectural stimulation.

The curious term 'deconstructivism' seems to suggest an architecture that takes buildings apart. In fact the word has linguistic roots in two cultural movements. First of all, it is related to the deconstructionist movement in 1970s' literary criticism, an attempt by literary scholars to take texts to pieces in order to excavate hidden meanings – meanings of which previous readers and even the authors of the texts were often quite unaware.

The second set of roots lies in the artistic movement called constructivism, which flourished in Russia in the 1920s (see pages 116–119). As well as being a type of architecture that embraced a particular kind of functionalist design, the Russian movement also involved design and painting, in which the paintings of El Lissitzky – which consisted of abstract arrangements of geometrical shapes and fragments – were especially prominent.

An architecture of fragmentation Deconstructivism in architecture draws to a certain extent on both of these origins, but is

timeline

1977

Frank Gehry designs the Gehry House, Santa Monica, California

very different from either. It creates buildings that often look fragmented, their parts and walls colliding at odd angles to produce odd, disjointed forms. Screens, beams, pillars and similar features create spaces that are half-inside, half-outside, so it is often difficult to tell where the boundaries of the structure are. The interiors often have an unusual sense of space, with odd angles and forms that challenge the traditional idea of a building as being full of rectangles.

The resulting sense of fragmentation in these buildings is sometimes influenced by Russian constructivist paintings, sometimes aims to analyse the building like a deconstructivist critic, but more often happens because of the specific vision of the architect.

Pivotal projects When the movement was launched in 1988 at an exhibition at the Museum of Modern Art in New York, the catalogue used terms such as dislocation, disruption, deflection and distortion to describe the type of buildings it would produce. At that point few deconstructivist buildings had actually been put up, but one exception was the adaptation of his own house the architect Frank Gehry undertook in 1977–78. The Gehry house turned from a simple bungalow into a bizarre structure fronted by additions that seem to recall sculptures made out of industrial materials such as mesh fencing, corrugated iron and concrete.

Another built project, the series of pavilions ('*Folies*') for the Parc de la Villette in Paris designed by Bernard Tschumi, also used a new and

> **❝Deconstructionist architecture ... works best as an exception within a strong defined norm.❞**
> **Charles Jencks**

1982–85	1988	1989
Bernard Tschumi's *Folies* for the Parc de la Villette, Paris, under construction	Deconstructivist exhibition is held at the Museum of Modern Art in New York	Daniel Libeskind begins work on the Jewish Museum, Berlin

disorientating sense of space and form. But Tschumi gave the buildings a type of unity by drawing on 1920s constructivist machinery for inspiration and by painting all the pavilions a bright, vibrant red.

Building and meaning

Many have doubted that buildings can embody the type of linguistic philosophy that deconstructivism apparently draws on. How easy it is to assign 'meaning' to these outwardly chaotic and bizarre buildings? In reply to this question, some architects, such as Bernard Tschumi, say that their buildings not only question the validity of conventional structures, but also reveal the fragmentation and disunity in modern culture. Another view sees buildings like the Gehry house (below) working in another way: their form can be viewed as offering a criticism of the more complacent designs generated by consumer society. Both views see deconstructivist architecture as embodying a radical alternative to the norm, and, as the architect and critic Charles Jencks has pointed out, this type of design is at its most powerful and relevant when it stands out as the exception to the rule.

Since then the various architects who have become known as deconstructivist have gone their separate ways, but many of them have made works with this sense of fragmentation. Frank Gehry has exploited computer design technology to create buildings, such as the famous Guggenheim Bilbao, that are all dramatic curves and reflections. Daniel Libeskind has used a new sense of space to symbolize the traumas of 20th-century history in his Jewish Museum, Berlin. The Viennese practice called Coop Himmelb(l)un has created an almost expressionist architecture out of deconstructivism's radical fragmentation and juxtapositions. Peter Eisenman, adept at reinventing himself, has produced diverse buildings, but his NC Building, Tokyo (which looks as if it is about to collapse) and his Aronoff Center, New York (resembling a set of toppling boxes) have explored deconstructivism's fascination with fragmentation.

Meanwhile one or two architects – notably Tschumi and Eisenman – continued to draw on the movement's intellectual roots, Eisenman seeing his buildings in part as intellectual exercises to benefit a late 20th-century landscape from which any sense of place or identity was fast vanishing.

Deconstructivism stimulated architects in several ways. It provided a healthy reaction against cynical commercial skyscrapers, against the ultra-smooth surfaces of high-tech and against the sometimes facile designs of postmodernism. It offered fresh ways of defining space and of thinking about buildings in symbolic terms. And it provided excitement in a period when burgeoning market capitalism seemed to demand designs that were visually boring – from mirror-faced office blocks to identikit shop fronts. The movement is still influencing architecture in these beneficial ways, stimulating prominent architects such as Zaha Hadid and Rem Koolhaas whose search for new forms is continuous and exciting.

the condensed idea
Dislocation, dislocation, dislocation

50 Green architecture

Architects are responding in different ways to issues surrounding carbon emissions, energy consumption and climate change. The resulting green architecture is partly about adopting the right materials and technologies, but basic concepts such as the correct orientation of buildings and sensitivity to site are equally important in creating buildings that are at once welcoming to occupants and low in their impact on the Earth and its resources.

Building is one of the most energy-intensive human activities. The construction process alone takes up large amounts of energy, materials and land, and buildings – the biggest objects we create – have a huge impact on their sites and surroundings. When we begin to occupy a building, the consumption of energy and the production of waste material continue.

The idea of green or sustainable architecture has emerged over the past few decades to address these issues. Green architecture aims to produce buildings that have a low impact on the environment while remaining attractive structures to look at and to use. The movement has produced very diverse buildings – there is no one visual style that is 'green'.

Roots and interests The roots of green architecture are spread wide. Inspiration comes partly from outside architecture – from those

timeline

1970s

Earthship Biotecture pioneer the use of recycled materials to create off-grid houses in southern USA

who have written and campaigned about environmental issues, for example. There are also architectural roots in the alternative architecture movement, which was producing self-sufficient, 'off-grid' buildings long before most of the world's population became aware of climate change (see pages 192–195).

Absorbing these influences and thinking deeply about the environmental impact of structures has led green architects and builders to concentrate on several main areas. The key preoccupations of green architecture can be summarized as: choice of materials, energy consumption and production, waste management and the relationship of building to site.

The Autonomous House

The architects Robert and Brenda Vale built this influential sustainable house in England in 1993. Much of the structure is faced with traditional bricks (fired with gas from decomposing rubbish) so that the house fits into its British town setting. But it uses highly thermally efficient masonry, including high-density concrete blocks, and large areas of multilayer glazing to keep the heat in. An array of solar panels produces electricity, sometimes generating a surplus, which the occupants sell to the grid. The house is also self-sufficient in water supply and waste management.

1972
The company LOG ID is founded in Germany to develop solar construction systems

1974
British architect Arthur Quarmby develops earth-sheltered building in Underhill, a house in Yorkshire

1993
Brenda and Robert Vale build their Autonomous House

Materials Green architects seek to use materials that have a low environmental impact. This can mean selecting local materials, to reduce the energy consumed in transportation – sustainably grown timber, straw bales and earth have all been used. It might mean using recycled resources, such as the car tyres and bottles used in Earthships (see pages 192–195). But it can equally mean utilizing conventional materials, such as concrete and glass, that are valued for their insulating or light-admitting qualities. In deciding on which materials to use, the architect is balancing their environmental impact with the qualities they will bring to the finished building – which in turn will have an environmental impact.

Energy Renewable energy sources are key. Green buildings often have solar panels, wind turbines and other methods of energy production built-in. But equally important are designing and orienting the building to make best use of sun and shade. A conservatory with a wall of glass might be positioned on the sunniest side of the building to gather heat and make best use of the sun in winter – but with some shading (overhanging roofs, blinds or even trees) to reduce glare in the summer. Correct orientation enables the building to make the best use of available sun and shade. In some climates, especially where there is a prevailing wind, orientation can help keep the building well ventilated or cool.

Green buildings are also designed to retain the heat they gather from the sun or generate on-site. Thick walls of materials such as rammed earth or straw bales help interiors stay warm in the winter and cool in the summer. If the walls are thinner, generous insulation can be fitted to achieve the same effect. Double or triple glazing also keep in heat.

Air flow

A large amount of energy is consumed in many modern buildings to power air-conditioning units. Green buildings normally eliminate air conditioning by appropriate orientation and the careful placing of vents and window openings. The shape of a building can also influence air flow.

Water and waste management A sustainable building is designed to reduce waste. The plumbing system often allows occupants to recycle waste water from washing machines or dish washing for flushing lavatories. Composting toilets are sometimes installed in green buildings, and users may also be encouraged to compost other household waste to feed the soil and reduce the amount of rubbish sent to landfill.

> **Whatever the nature of the site, I try to create architecture that is never imposing on its environment.**
>
> Tadao Ando, 'Reflections on Underground Space'

A diverse architecture Designing in this way has produced a fascinating body of green buildings across the world. Thinking in green terms has encouraged architects to experiment with new technologies, to look afresh at traditional materials, such as adobe, timber, bamboo and natural fibres, and to experiment with natural materials in new ways, as in straw-bale building.

It has also led some architects to develop the 'organic' architecture pioneered by Frank Lloyd Wright. Earth-sheltered buildings, structures in which the relationship between inside and outside are explored in new ways, houses that celebrate the 'elements' of earth, air, fire and water can all take on new 'green' forms.

Sensitivity to site, too, makes green buildings extremely diverse. They range from massive, earth-walled houses in Arizona to lightweight bamboo structures in Southeast Asia, from highly insulated timber houses in Scandinavia to glass and corrugated iron buildings in Australia. Sustainability offers both hope for the future and a new richness to architecture.

the condensed idea
Building can be good for the planet

Glossary

Aggregate Material (usually sand and/or stone) mixed with cement and water to make concrete.

Arch Structure, usually curved, of mutually supporting stones (or other pieces) spanning a gap.

Architrave Lowest of the three main parts of a classical entablature.

Atrium Covered courtyard-like area inside a building, usually lit from above by skylights.

Béton brut Concrete poured into a wooden mould and left untreated so that when the wood is removed the imprint of marks, such as the grain of the wood, remains on its surface.

Capital Crowning feature of a column.

Capsule In modern Japanese architecture, a self-contained module containing a whole room or apartment.

Cartouche Decorative moulded border, often in the form of an oval or scroll.

Cast iron Iron that has been melted and poured into a mould to produce a component, such as a column or railing.

Classicism Form of architecture based on the ideas of the ancient Greeks and Romans and the various styles derived from their buildings.

Cornice The upper, projecting section of an entablature; or any projecting moulding at the top of a wall.

Cottage orné House designed in a deliberately highly ornamental, rustic style with the use of features such as thatched roofs and rough-hewn or tree-like columns.

Curtain wall In modern architecture, a non-load-bearing wall, often consisting of glass, attached to the framework of a skyscraper.

Cylinder glass Window glass produced by producing a cylinder-shaped glass vessel, making a lengthways cut and flattening the material out to make a rectangular piece.

Earth-sheltered building Structure built partly underground or sheltered by earth banks, often with a turf- or earth-covered roof.

Entablature The upper part of an order, above the column and capital, consisting of a lintel made up of three variously moulded or ornamented layers: the architrave, frieze and cornice.

Faience Tin-glazed earthenware, used to make tiles or other types of applied architectural decoration.

Flying buttress Half-arch that takes the outward thrust of a vault or roof, transferring the force to lower supporting masonry.

Folly Small building in a landscape garden or park, built as an eyecatcher or to show the owner's eccentricity.

Free plan Plan in which, rather than having separate rooms, the internal spaces of a building merge into each other with minimal internal dividing walls.

Fresco Wall painting in which the pigment is applied directly to the plaster while the surface is still wet.

Frieze The middle, usually highly decorated, band of an entablature; more generally, any decorated band running along the upper part of a wall.

Functionalism The idea, common in modernist architecture, that a building's use and function should dictate the structure's physical form.

Gazebo Small garden building designed as a place from which to admire the view.

Geodesic dome Structure, usually hemispherical, made up of many lightweight rods joined together to form hexagons or other geometrical shapes; pioneered by Richard Buckminster Fuller.

Machine aesthetic Type of design that values unadorned, but beautifully finished, surfaces and components, which look as if they have been mechanically made.

Moderne Term used to describe both the highly decorative 1920s' Art Deco style and the similar, but less highly ornamented, streamline moderne style of the same period.

Modernism Term used generally to describe the various avant-garde movements in art and architecture in the early 20th century, especially those embracing new technology, the abandonment of ornament and the creation of buildings designed to reflect modern ways of life.

Module Standard unit of size, or prefabricated, standardized unit that can form part of a structure.

Moulding Continuous ornamented band running along a wall or around an arch or opening, designed either as decoration or to throw water away from a door or window.

Off-grid Term to describe a building that, being self-sufficient in terms of energy, is not connected to the normal energy-supply networks.

Order Set of design guidelines for columns and entablatures in classical architecture, normally conforming to one of five types: Doric, Ionic, Corinthian, Composite or Tuscan.

Palace front Façade (sometimes fronting several separate buildings, such as a terrace of houses) designed to resemble a single, grand neoclassical palace.

Pattern book Publication containing a series of illustrations of ideal buildings, plans, details and fittings, arranged so that a builder may copy them.

Pavilion Ornamental building, usually small or lightly constructed, and often used as a summerhouse; alternatively, a small, semi-independent protruding wing of a large building.

Pier Solid mass of masonry supporting an arch; usually more substantial than a column.

Pilaster Decorative strip protruding from a wall and usually resembling a flattened attached column.

Piloti Pillar used in modern architecture to raise a building above the ground to first-floor level.

Portico Entrance porch, usually supported by a row of columns, acting as the centrepiece to the façade of a classical building.

Ribbed vault Vault arranged as a series of compartments separated by a network of protruding ribs.

Romanesque The round-arched style of architecture, influenced by Roman building, fashionable between the 7th and 12th centuries.

Rustication Type of masonry made up of massive blocks (sometimes with a roughened surface) separated by deep joints.

Sharawaggi Term used in the 18th century to describe the asymmetrical design of gardens and buildings, derived from a similar asymmetry in oriental art.

Suspended structure Structure in which the main stresses are tensile; in tent-like structures, for example, the supporting masts are in compression but the fabric roofs and cables are in tension.

Sustainable Term used to describe a building designed to minimize the burden on the Earth's resources, through the use of recycled or renewable materials, the provision of power-generation resources and so on.

Trompe l'oeil Style of painting in which three-dimensional images are depicted with such precision that they seem to be real; used in the decoration of buildings, especially in baroque architecture.

Truss Frame, designed to span a space or support part of a structure such as a roof, and built up from parts in tension and compression.

Umbrello Small ornamental building designed to provide shelter in a garden.

Vernacular The type of buildings constructed in the traditional way, using local materials and resources, and not normally involving an architect.

Villa In Italian Renaissance and Palladian architecture, a country house or farmstead; in the picturesque movement, an asymmetrical country house; in later usage, a detached house, often in a town.

Zoning In planning, laying out a town or city in a way that allocates different functions to different areas, such as residential, industrial, commercial and administrative zones.

Index

Quercus Publishing Plc
55 Baker Street
7th Floor, South Block
London
W1U 8EW

First published in 2010

A catalogue record of this book is available from the British Library

UK and associated territories:
ISBN 978 1 84866 065 6
US and associated territories:
ISBN 978 1 84866 077 9

Printed and bound in China

10 9 8 7 6 5 4 3

Text by Philip Wilkinson

Prepared by Starfish Design, Editorial and Project Management Ltd.

Picture credits:
p5 illustration by PZ Art; p11 illustration by PZ Art; p13T. Bradford/iStockphoto; p14 illustration by PZ Art; p18 Jodie Coston/iStockphoto; p22 Georgio Magini/iStockphoto; p25 © 2006 Alberto Fernandez Fernandez/www.wikipedia.org/ Creative Commons licence/ http://creativecommons.org/ licenses/by-sa/3.0/; p29 Peter Willems/istock; p34 illustration by PZ Art; p38 © 2006 Photo by Fritz Saalfeld/www.wikipedia.org/Creative Commons licence/http:// creativecommons.org/licenses/by/2.5/; p41 Sebastian Julian/iStockphoto;p46 Simon Brown/Fotolia: p49 Amanda Lewis/iStockphoto; p51 Chechele/iStockphoto; p55 © 2006 Eneyama/www.wikipedia.org/Public Domain/http://en.wikipedia.org/wiki/ Public_domain; Don Bayley/iStockphoto; p57 Étienne-Louis Boullée, Cénotaphe a Newton (1784)/www.wikipedia.org/Public Domain/http://en.wikipedia.org/wiki/Public_domain; p61 © Barr Smith Library,The University of Adelaide; p65 Mitzy/shutterstock images; p70 © George P. Landow/victorianweb.org; p73 Nikos/iStockphoto; p78 © KoS/www.wikipedia.org/Creative Commons licence/http://creativecommons.org/licenses/by-sa/3.0/; p81 Andrew Kaupang/iStockphoto; p86 © 2006 Velela /www.wikipedia.org/Public Domain/http://en.wikipedia.org/wiki/Public_domain; p88 Library of Congress, Prints & Photographs Division, [reproduction number: LC-USZ62-104794] p94 Dave Elderfield/iStockphoto; p98 © Jacqueline Banerjee/victorianweb.org; p101 Courtesy of Otis Elevator Co.; p107 © Freepenguin/www.wikipedia.org/Creative Commons licence/http://creativecommons.org/ licenses/by-sa/3.0/; p109 © 2006 Aktron/www.wikipedia.org/Creative Commons licence /http://creativecommons.org/licenses/by-sa/3.0/; p114 © 2006 Ellywa/ www.wikipedia.org/Creative Commons licence /http://creativecommons. org/licenses/by-sa/3.0/; p118 Plates from the A.V. Shchusev State Research Museum of Architecture; Moscow; p122 © 2003 Detlef Mewes/www. wikipedia.org/public domain/http://en.wikipedia.org/wiki/Public_domain; p125 © 2003 Valueyou/www.wikipedia.org/Creative Commons licence/ http://creativecommons.org/licenses/by-sa/3.0/; p129 Jack E Boucher/ Library of Congress, Prints and Photographs Division, Historic American Buildings Survey, HABS: ILL,47-PLAN.V,1-8; p134 © 2008 Rwendland/ www.wikipedia.org/Creative Commons licence/http://creativecommons. org/licenses/by-sa/3.0/; p137 © 2004 Dan Smith /www.wikipedia.org/ Creative Commons licence/http:// creativecommons.org/licenses /by/ 2.5/;p142 Norman Pogson /iStockphoto; p147 Andrew Klafter/iStockphoto; p150 Ian Hamilton/ iStockphoto; p155 © Foofy /www.wikipedia.org/ Creative Commons licence/http://creativecommons.org/licenses/by/2.5/; p158 © Alessi; p163 © 2003 Brendan Williams/www.wikipedia.org/Creative Commons licence/http://creativecommons.org/licenses/by/2.5/; p166 © Chris73/www.wikipedia.org/Creative Commons licence/http:// creativecommons.org/licenses/by-sa/3.0/; p170 © 2009 Ozeye/www. wikipedia.org/Creative Commons licence/http://creativecommons.org/ licenses/by-sa/3.0/; p174 © 2007 Rob Lawson/www.wikipedia.org/Public Domain/http://en.wikipedia.org/wiki/Public_domain; p178 © 2008 Susleriel/www.wikipedia.org/Public Domain/http://en.wikipedia.org/ wiki/Public_domain; p181 © Venturi, Scott Brown and Associates, Inc. p186YinYang/iStockphoto; p191 © 2005 Andrew Dunn/www.wikipedia. org/ Creative Commons licence/http://creativecommons.org/licenses/by-sa/2.0/; p195 AlanDJ/iStockphoto; p198 © 2007 IK/www.flickr.com/Creative Commons licence/http://creativecommons.org/licenses/by/2.0/ deed.en_GB; p201 © Robert Vale.